# 6 Minutes

# Wrestling With Life

JohnA Passaro

# To BettyJane

Divided by location.
United by cause.
Bonded by love and belief.

# Other Books by JohnA Passaro

**"Again"** (Book 2) – The Sequel to **"6 Minutes Wrestling With Life"**

There are going to be many occasions where you are faced with giving up.

Where the normal person would not hold it against you for stopping.

Where almost everyone would give you a pat on the back for a most valiant effort.

It is at that time that you have a choice to make.

You could accept the alibi that is being thrown to you,

Or you can try "Again."

Give all of us gathered here tonight

The strength to remember that life is so fragile.


We are all vulnerable.


And we will all, at some point in our lives…fall.


We will all fall.


We must carry this in our hearts…


That what we have is special.

That it can be taken from us.


And when it is taken from us,

We will be tested.

We will be tested to our very souls.

We will now all be tested.

It is these times.

It is this pain

That allows us to look inside ourselves.


Coach Eric Taylor

Friday Night Lights

# Table of Contents

# Foreword

So I knew a guy in high school who was one of those people who just seemed to have something different about him.

Different in a good way.

Different in a way that made you admire him, but you didn't really know why.

He was a regular guy in a lot of ways. He wasn't a big guy, or a super fast guy. In fact he was more or less very average in most every category.

He was definitely a very good, very dedicated athlete, but not necessarily the best player on the team.

He was a starter on every team he played on. He played baseball and soccer and was clearly one of the core players on both teams. But generally, I would say if you were asked to rate him as a player you would say he was closer to "very good" than "great".

But wrestling was his thing.
He was an insanely dedicated wrestler.
Like crazy, off the charts, lunatic, kind of dedicated....

I remember thinking he was out of his mind to work that hard at something so gritty and (seemingly) unglamorous. All the hours spent in that dark, dirty, musty, wrestling room through the cold and gloom of winter. Not to mention "sucking weight" constantly. I remember thinking the pain and suffering and dedication was going 24 hours a day instead of just the three or four hours of practice in that pit.

I also remember admiring the living crap out him for doing it.

I never mustered up the guts to tell him back then, but down deep I wished I had half of his focus and determination.

This guy was funny, he was smart, and he was quick with a smile.

He was pretty much like anyone you might have known in high school.

Except for one thing.

Nobody **EVER** out worked him.
I remember one day after school someone challenged him to do a thousand sit-ups.

A THOUSAND sit-ups.

Back when we all thought 50 was a lot.

Back when "3 sets of 10" gave you stomach cramps the next day.

Old school sit-ups, not those bs crunches.

So anyway, he didn't do it.... Unfortunately, nobody would walk the halls the following day and talk about watching him knock out 1,000 sit-ups....

Because when he got to 1,226 sit-ups the janitor wanted to go home.

ONE THOUSAND, TWO HUNDRED, AND TWENTY-FRIGGIN-SIX SIT-UPS.

You see, the truth is you never know what lies within someone.

People are capable of inexplicable strength and determination seemingly way beyond what you "expect" of them. Some people ignore 'physics' and decide it doesn't apply to them. They don't subscribe to this thing most of us call "logic". To people like this, logic and conventional wisdom doesn't help change the world. To them, those two things will never serve you well when you face seemingly insurmountable odds.

So anyway, I lost touch with this guy the day we walked away from our graduation ceremony. We weren't super close and life pulled us into our respective directions.

Thirty years later I came across him because of this book that he wrote.

A book about the triumphs and tragedies he has faced in his life.

I wasn't surprised at all to find out that this insanely dedicated athlete/wrestler (and now father) had gone on to motivate, cajole, and coach his first son into a State Champion wrestler for Eastport South Manor High School on Long Island in 2012. (The school's first ever, state champion) From what I have seen, he is also well on his way to repeating that with his second son as I type this story.

The only thing more powerful, more impactful, or more life changing than the highs he has faced in his life has been the lows that he has been dealt.

He was handed an unthinkable tragedy with his eldest daughter.

And this is where the toughness and conviction of that wrestler, who would have done a million sit-ups if that janitor didn't have to go home, called upon his own unrivaled focus and determination and took a pass at saying "Uncle".

Where "What Lies Within" took on a whole new definition for me...

Thank you John Passaro for your strength, conviction, and inspiration. You have absolutely no idea how much I (still) admire you.

I am positive Jess is proud to call you dad....

Fight on brother.

**Steve Marshall**

# Chapter 1

# How Long Is - For a While?

I don't know if we each have a destiny,

Or if we're all just floating around

Accidental-like on a breeze.

But I think maybe it's both.

Maybe both are happening at the same time.


Forrest Gump

**August 21st, 2009**

"Jess, why don't you come sit down and watch this movie with us?"
I asked my daughter in an attempt to spend more time with her
before she headed back to college in a few days for her sophomore
year at FIT.

"It's Serendipity, with John Cusack."

"I think I am just going to go to sleep for a while…"
Jess said as she spun herself around the wooden bannister and
headed up the stairs to her bedroom.

That didn't sound right…

Usually Jess would say, "I'm going to bed – goodnight," why did she say, "I'm going to go to sleep for a while?

That was weird.

Without anything else to go on, other than my parental radar, I dismiss the slight change in her "good night" wording and convince myself that Jess is just tired after coming home from a ten-hour shift at work, where she has worked the whole summer in a retail fashion boutique in the Hampton's.

In a few seconds my parental radar's antenna comes back down to earth and I get consumed with the movie once again.

"Serendipity, it is one of my favorite words.  It is just a nice sound for what it means *a fortunate accident.*  Except I don't really believe in accidents, I believe fate is behind everything… I think fate sends us little signs and it is how we read those signs that determine whether we are happy, or not."

BOOM.

"What was that?" – I ask my wife, BettyJane as I immediately do what any normal person does when they hear a noise in the middle of the night – I wait for the second noise to confirm that I heard the first noise.

There is nothing but an eerie silence.

I am still not convinced that the silence negated the first boom, so I get up and put on the outside lights to the house.

I look outside.
Everything seems fine.

I check the garage - everything looks normal.

No other noises.

I'm satisfied that there is no home invasion in process, the car is not being robbed and my family is safe, so I sit back down on the couch to continue watching the movie.

As soon as I sit down, I hear the second, louder noise – this time **A THUD.**

BettyJane jerks up off of the couch and dashes upstairs, instinctively yelling JESS! JESS! JESS!

We didn't know it at the time, but the first **BOOM** was Jess losing her balance and falling into her closet door, and the second **THUD** was her closet door collapsing and hitting the wall, and sliding to the ground.

I follow BettyJane and her instinctive motherly hysteria up the stairs.

We both get up the stairs at the same time and we see our twelve-year-old son Travis holding his sisters limp body in his arms, in the hallway of her bedroom.

As soon as Travis sees my wife and me, he drops his sister's body and backs up to the edge of the wall, like someone would do after they disbelievingly shot someone and stood over the dead body.

He is in shock.

Ahh Jess.

Ahh Jess.

Ahh Jess.

I remember saying over and over again as I tried to lift Jess's limp body from the ground. Her body is like liquid Silly Putty, every time

I try and lift her – her body finds an opening and plunks to the floor without any form.
Call 911!

Call 911!

Call 911!

Travis is motionless.

Call 911!

Call 911!

Call 911!

My seven-year-old daughter, Cassidy appears on the top of the stairs with our house phone. My wife yanks it from her small hands and starts dialing for help…

I momentarily look up and think to myself that Cassidy, standing on the stairs looking at what is happening, looks as innocent as Cindy Lu Who when she saw the Grinch stealing the last bulb on the tree, on Christmas Eve.

And just like the Grinch, I think up a lie, and I think one up quick: "Jess is just not feeling well – why don't you just go downstairs, we will be down in a while." I tell her as deceptively as the Grinch said to Cindy Lu.

She looks back at me as disbelieving as Cindy Lu Who looked at the Grinch as he slithered up the chimney.

As I am speaking to Cassidy, out of the corner of my eye, I see Jess attempting to use the wall to gain enough balance to stand.
She can't.

But she creates enough room between her body and the wall that makes an opening for me to insert my arm to help her up.
I get her up. She leans on me. Her face is six inches from mine. Her beautiful hazel green eyes have turned morbidly black with dilation.

Ahh Jess.

Ahh Jess.

Ahh Jess.

Jess's body starts shaking, trembling. She is seizing. Her eyes roll back into her head – all I see now is the whites…. Her body gets real stiff. I feel like that if I were to move her, I would break her.

"I got to go – I got to go…" I yell out.

I bend down, put my left arm between Jess's legs, while my right arm grabs her elbow, and I put her in a fireman's carry hold and I run with her down the stairs.

"Be careful, don't slip, don't slip – take each stair," I say to myself as I run frantically down the stairs.

I get to the bottom of the stairs.

Her body feels different.

Heavier.

She is covering more of my back and less of my shoulders at this point.

I kneel down and gently lower my head to take her body off of my back and shoulders and onto the icy tile floor in front of my front door.

She has stopped breathing.

Ahh Jess.

I immediately pinch her nose, open her mouth and start performing CPR.

This is not happening, I am thinking to myself as I am blowing air into her mouth…

I put my right palm onto my left thumb and I start pressing on her chest.

Nothing.

I keep repeating the process for what feels like forever.

I feel a tap on my shoulders and hear: "We'll take over from here."

The EMT's are here – thank God.

They open up their EMT medical box, apply oxygen and something to Jess's chest and within a few seconds they have her breathing again.

Wow.  That was scary.

A few minutes go by and Jess seems to be coming too.

I walk outside for some air and to stabilize myself from the events from the last few minutes.

I hear: "Hey buddy, buddy over here."

There are two Police Officers who are waving me over to them. I walk over to them.

One of the officers puts his arm around me, starts to walk me in a direction away from the other officer and says:

"Hey buddy – the next time you call 911 make sure someone is not breathing, you hear?"
And he walks away as if I annoyed him.

I didn't have time to say "F&*k You" to the officer, as I see my daughter being brought out of my house, and down my front stoop stairs on a gurney. The EMT's are not rushing, they are calm and they are by her side. They head toward the ambulance in the street, which awaits them.

I think to myself, a tragedy has been averted.
Why else would the officer say that to me, if we were not out of the woods?

"Is anyone driving in the ambulance with us?" the EMT inquires to BettyJane and me.

It immediately dawns on me. Maverick, my fifteen-year-old son is not home and we need to call someone to come over to watch Cassidy and Travis (who is still in shock).

"Call Rich and Terri" – I yell to my wife as she is lifting her leg to get into the back of the ambulance.

"Ok – I will. I will meet you at the hospital. Don't stop for Jujubes."
BettyJane says as the ambulance back door slams shut and she disappears.

Things have to be OK if she is quoting Seinfeld- right?

When I get to the hospital, Jess has already been transported into a partition in the Emergency Room; BettyJane is outside of that partition looking in, as five doctors are working on Jess.

They seem to have her stabilized.

21

Everything is under control.

A few minutes go by, both BettyJane and I are watching every move inside of the room.
Doctors start leaving the room, one at a time.
In a few minutes time the last doctor leaves the room.

That is a good sign.

Now there are only a few nurses in the room with Jess.

They start leaving also.

Now there is just one nurse in the room. Jess is stable.

Wow – that was scary.

BettyJane and I continue watching the one nurse in the room.
She picks up an IV Medical bag and hangs it from Jess's medical pole, which is attached to her arm.

She leaves the room also.

Jess must be stable if she doesn't need anyone by her side, I think to myself.

Twenty seconds goes by.

DING, DING, DING, DING…

Every bell and red alert starts to go off and Jess is violently shaking on the bed. Her head goes up and down violently hitting the mattress many multiple times.

A swarm of doctors and nurses rush into the room.

What just happened?

BettyJane rushes into the room and confronts the nurse who hung the medicine on Jess's pole.
"What did you give her?"

"What did you give her?"

She gets no reply, so she rushes to the garbage pail where one of the doctors has unhooked the IV bag and tossed it away.

"What is this?"

"What is this?"

She asks as she picks up the IV bag out of the garbage.

A doctor walks up to her, takes the bag from her hand and escorts her out of the room saying – "We need to work on your daughter now."

BetytyJane obliges and comes by my side outside of the room.
As I look into the room, I see the frantic pace that everyone in that room is operating at, and I realize that I have entered a place where no person ever wants to be.

I have entered hell.

My wife realizes this also.

NOOOOOOOO
NOOOOOOOOOOO

NOOOOOOOOOOOOOOO

She offers up a deal to the Gods...

"TAKE ME INSTEAD"

"TAKE ME INSTEAD"

There is nothing more blood curdling than a mother's cry and scream when their child is in danger.

I look up and I see that the nurse behind the ER desk is crying…

At that moment, BettyJane decides to sacrifice herself to the gods in replacement of her daughter.  She decides to do a Tosh.O trust fall, with no one behind her to catch her, to seal the deal.
Luckily I am within five feet of her when she decides to do this and somehow I avert her crashing backwards, head first to the floor.

I lift her up, catching her just inches from the floor.
Her body is limp and she is repeating the words "I'm OK", "I'm OK".
I know that she is playing possum with me hoping that I would leave her alone so she could attempt the trust fall again without me being there.  I am wise to her strategy and I hold her in my arms.  She sinks though my arms and withers to the floor.

"Get the white curtains." A doctor commands.

"Get the white curtains and Close the ER!"

"Move everyone out of the ER – NOW!"

Did he just say: "Close the ER?"

The nurse at the ER desk, who has to be a mother also, is overwhelmed with a sense of powerlessness as she has the same look on her face that Patrick Swayze had in Ghost right before the spirits arrived.

I immediately sense it.

Ohhh noo.  NOOOO I yell.

I force BettyJane to sit in a chair to avert another attempt to sacrifice herself.

It has been 2 minutes since the red alert.

A Jamaican Priest walks over to me and says:
"I would like to administer last rights to your daughter before she dies in a few minutes.  Without it, she will not be able to get into heaven."

I look him square in the eyes and say: "If you don't get out of here I am going to kill you, and you will be the one needing last rights."

He continues and continues and continues – he puts his hand on my shoulder and starts saying "Forgive him Lord, he knows not what he is doing."

I reply – "I know exactly what I am doing, and I am giving you a five second head start."

He moves away.

I look up and I see my mother and mother in law walk into the ER.

There is terror on their faces.  I now have three people to console.

The priest now attempts to convince my mother, who is a Eucharistic Minister, to allow him to administer last rights.  She tells him "To get away from her before she punches him."
He moves on.

It has been 3 minutes now.

Come on, come on…

This can't be happening.

4 Minutes…
5 Minutes…

6 Minutes…

It's over I thought.

Wait - I see movement from inside the room. I can hear them talking.

Please don't say it – just don't say it.

Just don't say "Time of Death."

The doctor is coming out – I brace myself for what I feel has to be the inevitable speech: "I am sorry we tried everything that we could…"

Dr. Clarence walks out – me and my wife have nicknamed him that because he looks like the Angel from "It's a Wonderful Life", and he says: "We went well beyond what we should have done, she is an eighteen year old girl, we tried everything we could to save her."

No No  No  No  No  No

But he then said: "We had to put her into a medically induced coma, it is the best that we could do."

"A medically induced coma?"

I'll take it – ten seconds ago I thought Jess was dead.
"Does she have at least a 1% chance doctor?"

"Yes, she has a 1% chance."

"How long will she be like this, doctor?"

"I don't know," he replied.

"For a while."

# Chapter 2

# Every Breath is Gold

What every long shot,

Come from behind underdog

Will tell you is this:

The other guy may in fact be the favorite,

The odds may be stacked against you,

Fair enough.

But what the odds don't know is

This isn't a math test.

This is a completely different kind of test.

One where PASSION

Has a funny way of trumping logic.

No matter what the stats may say,

And the experts may think,

And the commentators may have predicted,

When the race is on all bets are off.

Versus Commercial

**August 22nd, 2009**

When you Google brain injuries you will quickly learn the grim statistics: A patient has 28 days to recover from the initial injury or their chances of a full recovery drop to less than 1%.

I immediately take inventory of the situation and my mind quickly translates it into a sports metaphor; that is just how my brain operates.

"I have just been sacked at my own 1 Yard line. There are 28 seconds on the clock and we are down by 8."

"Down by 8? " I ask myself.

"Yes, Down by 8." I answer.

"Ok, ok – down by 8." I accept the challenge and immediately start putting a plan into action…

"What we need to do is to go into our two minute offense, drive 99 yards for a touchdown and then convert a two point conversion to put the game into overtime, and win it there." The thought goes through my mind as if I were the quarterback in the huddle giving out instructions to myself on how I was going to take my daughter from a 1% chance of survival back up to a 100% chance again.

"Doug Flutie did it – right?" I say to myself.

"Why can't I?"

My mind immediately replays the ending to the infamous 1984 game in my head (I have watched this video over a hundred times over the years.)

*"Here we go here's your ballgame folks."*
*"The ballgame is on the line. Flutie and Boston College are on the 50 yard line with :06 to go, down by four."*

*"Three wide receivers out to the right..."*
*"Flutie takes the snap. He drops straight back, has some time, now he scrambles away from one hit, looks, uncorks a deep one to the end zone, as :00 seconds flashes on the screen.*

*Phelan is down there.*

*Ohhh he got it, did he get it?*

*He got it.*

*TOUCHDOWN! TOUCHDOWN! TOUCHDOWN! TOUCHDOWN Boston College.*

*He did it!*

*He did it!*

*Flutie did it – he hit Phelan in the end zone.*

*I don't believe it!*

*Oh my Goodness. What a play – Flutie to Phelan for 48 yards with no time on the clock.*

*Boston College wins 47-45,"* Dan Davis the announcer says.

I remember seeing an interview with Gerard Phelan, the Boston College wide receiver who caught the winning Hail Mary pass thrown by Doug Flutie.  I remember him saying, "When we were in the huddle, I don't think if you asked anybody they would have said this game is over. I think if you would have asked everybody they would have said "Hey wait a minute – we got another play. We got another chance to score a touchdown. And everybody went to work."

This is exactly what I am going to do.

There is still time on the clock.

I'm going to fight.

I'm going to win.

As soon as I got to the end of my mental imagery of all of the Boston College football team swarming over Gerard Phelan in the end zone, I am taken back into current time when I am summoned over to Jess's Neurologist:

"Mr. Passaro, could I speak with you for a second?" He has Jess's CT Scan results in his hands.

I walk over to him.

He extends his right hand out and invites me to shake hands.

I accept.

He extends the shake and puts his left hand on my forearm for affect.

A few seconds go by.

He is still gripping my hand.

The shake is no longer a shake, but rather a brace, as he holds onto my arm and says:

"Mr. Passaro, have you ever heard of Karen Ann Quinlan?"

I immediately, and not very politely, remove my hand from his grip, just like George Bailey did when he almost made a deal with Potter in "It's a Wonderful Life."

"Yes I have."

"Well, Mr. Passaro, I am sorry to inform you that I have reviewed your daughters CT Scan and she has no brain activity, just like in the

Karen Ann Quinlan case. At this time I want you to start thinking about the quality of her life."

"What do you mean – "Start thinking about the quality of her life?" I slowly and reluctantly inquire.

"Well, Mr. Passaro, she can stay attached to those machines in there for a long time, would you really want that?" He said, as he nudged his head in the direction of my daughters ICU room where Jess has so many tubes attached to her that I could barely recognize her.

"Doctor, I believe it is my job for me to fight for my daughters survival, not prepare for her death. Isn't that, what I, as her father, am supposed to do? Isn't that what you would do?"

"I don't agree Mr. Passaro, I believe you should really consider the quality of life that your daughter will have and prepare yourself to make some very difficult decisions."

I look into Jess's room, I see numbers flashing on my daughter's machine screens, and I think to myself – there is time for another play.

Beaten up and battered, I walk back into my daughters ICU room and in frustration I walk up to Jess's bed and I say to my daughter: "Jess, if you don't start moving pretty soon I am going to check your body for tattoos!" She knew I was not a fan of tattoos, especially ones that may be on her body.

The numbers on Jessica's computer monitor which monitored her heart rate start increasing.

128

142

156

"Does anyone see that?" I ask.

"I guess she doesn't want you to know." The nurse says as she is bending over putting some supplies in a cabinet.

"Know what?" I reply.

"That she has tattoos." She says as she moves towards Jess on the bed.

"I saw them when I was changing her." "You see, here they are." She said as she picked up Jess's hospital gown to show me.

"The first one is on her left side and is of a beautiful owl."

"And the second one…" she starts to say.

"The second one?" I disbelievingly utter.

"Yes, the second one is some writing under her right breast over here."

And there it was, my answer to any internal conflict of whether I was doing the right thing by fighting for Jess's life.

There on Jess's ribs were the words:

*"Every Breath is Gold."*

It is time to find my Gerard Phelan in the end zone.

# Chapter 3

# Divided, Yet United

United we stand.

Divided we fall.

Aesop

**August 25th, 2009**

It seems like it has been forever.

But I get the feeling that forever hasn't even started yet…

It is now Tuesday August 25th, 6:00 am, 80 hours since BettyJane and I have entered hell, and one day before BettyJane and my 20th wedding anniversary.

We have both been by Jess's side together, without an ounce of sleep, for every second of the last 80 hours. I know that sounds impossible, but it is true. The thought of Jess waking up and us being asleep has kept us both up to the point of mental and physical exhaustion.

I think to myself that this strategy is not going to work, that we are on a path for disaster. If we continue doing what we are doing, both BettyJane and I will burn out and no one will be able to be with Jess. We both realize that we are in for a long battle, so we reformulate a new plan. It is decided that BettyJane will take days 9 am-9 pm (so I can work days) and I will take nights from 9 pm – 9 am. (So BettyJane can get the kids ready for school each day.) It is agreed on that we will do whatever it takes to win this battle, even if it means that we will never see each other again in the process. That seems like a small price to pay in order to keep our family intact.

BettyJane and I have a deep emotional conversation about how a sick child can rip parents apart. How I have seen parents who lose a child, die inside and stop living altogether. How their other children are affected and how a person's attitude and belief system are attacked under these circumstances, and how if we don't protect ourselves from the ensuing attack how it could impact the rest of our lives, and more importantly our children's lives.

We make a commitment to each other that we will be divided in location, yet united in our cause.

That getting Jess better and losing our other three kids lives in the process is unacceptable, as is giving up on Jess and having our other kids live happily ever after, as if nothing has happened, is also, just as equally unacceptable to us.

We want both.

To care for and cure Jess, and to live and love life.

One without the other is unacceptable.

We want to invest every ounce of our energies to getting Jess better and we want our other kids to live life to the fullest.

Notice I did not say - live a normal life. As we know our lives will never be normal again.

We commit to each other that we will live two lives at the same time, giving each their proper attention and passion. We both understand the herculean effort that is going to be required to do this and we commit to each other that we will never falter in our cause.

We take our new vows to each other:
No matter what.
Good or bad.
Thick or thin.
Right or wrong.

It is at this moment that I realize the best thing I ever did in my life was to marry this woman.
She is willing to give up her life for her child. I know most parents would do the same. But how many mothers would give up everything that they love, everything that they will ever be able to do in the future for the "possibility and not the guarantee" of getting their child better.

Now reduce the odds of success to less than 1%.

How many mothers are still standing?

BettyJane is.

Being that it is 6:00 am, I am the one who gets to go home first.

Home.

It seems so distant.

So much has happened in just a short period of time.

My thoughts wonder to my life and everything that I was trying to accomplish, before four days ago.

How meaningless it all seems now.

I catch myself on my mental aberration and I promise to myself that I will not let that happen again. Life is full of meaning and is unbelievably awesome.

I am back on course.

My mind wanders to Travis; I wonder how he is doing?....
To Maverick, does he even know what happened; I haven't spoken to him yet...
To Cassidy, no seven year old should ever see what she saw.

My mind wanders to the thought of how their lives will change and how wrong that really is.

It is at this moment that I make a promise to myself to never stop until I achieve both.

To care for and cure Jess, and to live and love life.

I make it out to my truck, which is sitting alone in the hospital parking lot, under a light post.

I open the door to my vehicle, I step up into the drivers seat, put my hands on the steering wheel, and I let my head fall forward hitting the steering wheel, and I stay that way for a few moments.
I then lean my head back in the other direction, trying to take in the enormity of the last 80 hours.

I insert the key into the ignition, instinctively turn on the radio, hit the first preset and I let the torture begin:

*"How the hell'd we wind up like this?*
*Why weren't we able?*
*To see the signs that we missed."*

I quickly Click to preset #2:

*"One day you'll see it can happen to me.*
*I need a miracle.*
*I wanna be your girl..."*

Click.

*"As my memory rests.*
*But never forgets what I lost*
*Wake me up when September ends."*

I click off the radio, and look around as if someone is punking me.

A good feeling comes over me as I remember that the boys have a private wrestling lesson with Mike Patrovich in two hours. I have just enough time to go pick them up and make the half hour trip to Commack.

Yes, I am taking them to their wrestling private lesson.

I want BOTH.

They are both going to win a State Championship.

This goal has now become even more important to me, but now for a different reason. This is now the bogey for accomplishing one half of "I want both."

I give a quick departing glance up to Jess's room up on the third floor before I put the car in drive. Her room is on the corner of the building. I see BettyJane inside the room with her face in the palms of her hands, and just outside the room, perched on top of the roof as a decoration, there is a metal owl.

I cry.

# Chapter 4

# Gap Soldiers

Roger Bannister not only broke the record

For the fastest mile,

He also broke down the walls of impossibility.

As soon as Roger Bannister

Ran a sub 4-minute mile,

Many other runners soon did it also.

Because they believed that it was possible.

**August 25th, 2009**

I need to dream.

I need to believe.

I need to know that I have some control in my life.

That if I work hard, that I will be rewarded.

That life is not arbitrary.

I need to believe that bad things happen to good people, for a greater reason.

That dedication, sacrifice, hard work, discipline are all worthy attributes that will eventually produce extraordinary results.

That if I live a certain lifestyle, that my family will be better for that.

That there is a direct link between my actions and my results.

That If I prepare properly that I can face the insurmountable foe and look him in the eye and say "Bring it on, I can take whatever you can dish out."

I need to keep living in order to save my daughter from dying.

That is why, on zero hours sleep over the last four days, I finally put my truck in drive and I leave the hospital parking lot.

That is why I am taking my two sons to wrestling practice today.

That is why wrestling has become even more important to me.

There are very few places on this earth that I feel totally at home, that I can be myself, that I truly have a deep affection for the people that I am around, and that I crave to be at all times.

The basement of the old P.C. Richards Building in Commack, which is the home of the "Razor Wrestling Club", is one of those places.

I arrive at the club with Maverick and Travis and head down the basement stairs.

The place has an old boxing gym feel.

As we head down the stairs my right hand skims the wall as a guide. There is a huge chunk of concrete missing in the wall.

My hand automatically and instinctively lifts itself up before the hole and drops itself back down onto the wall right after the hole ends as I walk down the stairs.

I have literally done this over four hundred times over the last two years. For four days a week, for the last two years, it is at this basement at Razor Wrestling where you would have been able to find me.

I open the door to the basement gym. I see Mike Patrovich is sitting on the wrestling mat, against a steel beam, writing on a chalkboard with a marker, preparing for the upcoming lesson.

"Hey guys, how's it going, how was your weekend?" he asks…

Maverick, as he is putting on his wrestling shoes, looks up at me with a look that says, "How are you going to answer that?"

An electrical current of guilt runs through my body and I immediately think to myself: "What the hell am I doing here, what am I crazy."

Mike lifts his head and see's Mav looking at me strange and says:

"What?"

"What happened?"

I hesitate, but then I detail my last four days of my life to Mike, and I confess at the end: "I am feeling really guilty for being here right now, I just feel like crawling up in a ball, but I just had to come."
"It may be wrong, but I just need to be here," I added.

Mike immediately puts me at ease and says: "I know exactly what you are talking about."

He then tells me the real life story of when he was wrestling in college at Hofstra University, and his coach Tom Ryan, the current coach of Ohio State, had his five-year-old son Teague die in his arms in 2004.

Mike went on to say how wrestling helped Tom deal with that rough time in his life the best way that he knew how. Mike conveyed to me how much respect and admiration that he had for his former coach.

As Mike is speaking to me, my mind drifts back a few months to when Tom Ryan held a wrestling clinic at our high school. He was DYNAMIC, full of life and had the greatest attitude in a person that I have ever seen.

I am astounded. That can't be the same person that Mike is referring to. He assures me that it is.

Mike then suggests to me that I watch a videotape of a speech Tom recently gave at a ceremony naming the Hofstra wrestling room, the "Teague Ryan Wrestling Room." I make a mental note to watch the video as soon as I get home.

For the next sixty minutes Mikes takes the boys a step closer to a State Championship.

How many more steps will be needed? I don't know, but what I do know is that today they did the work necessary in order to one day make that goal a reality. And tomorrow they will do the same.

At the end of the sixty minutes, I thank Mike for all that he has done for me and the boys today and I head directly home to watch the video.

"Life teaches us that parents aren't supposed to say goodbye to their children." Tom Ryan starts out in the video. "I would give anything for it to be reversed."

He goes on to say, during his speech, that one of the keys to success is: "An unconditional commitment. A willingness to do whatever it takes, not under your own set of rules, but rather what is truly required."

He adds: "That an attitude and belief system of eternal optimism is everything."

I am listening to and watching the computer screen as if he is speaking directly to me.

Tom goes on to tell the story of the Gap Soldier:

*"A Gap Soldier lived in the times of Castles. A Gap Soldier was a well-trained soldier, who during an attack would walk through a break in the castle wall and hold off the enemy as they tried to rush in. They clearly knew what was at stake. I can't imagine the commitment of running through the hole in the wall preventing the enemy from coming in. It gets worse for the Gap Soldier. The bad news for the Gap Soldier was that while he fought the enemy outside the castle preventing them from coming in, his fellow soldiers were sealing up the castle behind him."*

I realize that BettyJane and I are now Gap Soldiers for our family.

He continues:
*"How hard are we willing to fight for what we want?*

*What sacrifices are we willing to make to achieve the things that we want?*

*Gap soldiers are an example of what we are capable of when we are fighting for something dear to us."*

I am mesmerized by the video and spend the next few hours reading stories about Tom Ryan and how he has dealt with the tragic loss of his son.

In one he starts off a speech saying: "I have four kids, three are alive." In another story he talked about despair: "Despair is a deep hurt that no human can fathom, until you are there." And adds: "The pain never goes away."

I find quote after quote of every emotion that I am currently experiencing.

Tom says in one interview "No one has caused me to hunger for the truth of life more than Teague has."

"The purpose of life, began at his death…"

There are not too many people who you meet for a brief few minutes in your life that can change your life for the better.

For me, Tom Ryan is one of those rare people who did.

When you know that something is possible, it is easier to accomplish. Tom Ryan has become my Roger Bannister.

Without ever "meeting with him" Tom Ryan made me realize that even through an unimaginable loss, one can still be dynamic, inspiring and keep their love for life. His unbelievable attitude and approach on life set an example of how I wanted to live my life.

Without him ever knowing it, he has become my guiding light.

I now know, that it is possible to live while you are dying inside.

I believe again.

# Chapter 5

# Follow the Love, Jess

The intuitive mind is a sacred gift

And the rationale mind is a faithful servant.

We have created a society

That honors the servant

And has forgotten the gift.


Albert Einstein

After reading every article that I could find on Tom Ryan, it is now approaching 6:00 pm.

It is time to relieve BettyJane.

I have now been up for ninety-two straight hours.

I arrive at the hospital during visiting hours for the ICU.

There are many family and friends in the waiting room all waiting to visit with BettyJane, myself and Jess.

For the next two hours, one at a time, friend after friend comes into Jess's room.  BettyJane will not leave. She talks too, hugs and cries with every visitor.

At 8:00 pm, the ICU nurse pokes her head into Jess's room and says: "I hate to do this, but visiting hours are over, please wrap up your visit."

BettyJane and I are currently visiting with Liz, Jessie's boss at work. Liz was the last person who spent the day with Jess before this occurred.  Disbelief, tears, and empathy are all flowing from Liz as she visits with us.

Once again the nurse politely asks us to wrap up the visitation.

BettyJane and Liz decide to walk out to their cars together.

BettyJane and I hug, a long extended hug, and finally there is the double tap from me on her back.

It is time to go home, I tell her.

They both start to walk toward the door to leave.

And just before walking out the door, Liz turns around, and just like Columbo says: "Just one more thing…"

"Mr. Passaro, you should know that Jess loved that talk that you guys had the other day.  She told me about it at work on Friday.  She said it was special."

I watch BettyJane and Liz leave the ICU together.

The talk. Oh my God.

Never have I ever had a talk with my Jess like I did the other day.

My mind reflects back to the talk.

"Dad, I am never going to have kids." Jess says as she sat down in a chair next to me while I was working from home the other day.

"Jess, don't say that – you love kids.  Don't worry you will eventually find the right guy, you will fall in love, settle down and you will start a family one day," I respond back to her, totally misreading her statement to me.

"No dad, *I know* that I am not going to have kids," she says to me.

"How do you know that?" I inquire.

"I can't explain it, I just have this feeling.  I just know."

"Dad – have you ever had one of those feelings?"

"Yes Jess, I know I am going to write one day.  I know that it seems unlikely right now, but I have always knew that I would write someday."

"You see that's the feeling that I am talking about.  It doesn't make sense, it seems improbable, but you just know."

"Dad, do you believe in heaven?" Jess asks.

"Jess, why do I get the feeling that this is not about what I believe – that it is really about what you believe? Do you believe in heaven?"

After a delay she says: "Yea, I do," and she throws out another question to me: "Why do you think that God let's bad things happen? Why doesn't he step in and fix things?"

"Jess, I don't have the answer to that question.  I have often wondered that myself," I reply.

"Do you think that there really is a God, then? Or do you think it is something that humans have made up to try and explain what they can't explain?" She goes on: "I don't know if I really believe that

Jesus was born from a virgin, that he walked on water and that he rose from the dead."

I try my best to have her keep her faith, while having the freedom to question it by asking: "Jess, let me ask you one question – Do you believe in love?"

"Of course I do – it is what everyone lives for," she shares with me.

"Well then Jess, I believe that God is love," I say.

"Just follow the love, Jess and everything else will fall into place."

"That is the best advice that I can ever give you, Jess. Just follow the love and everything will eventually be ok."

"I like that – "*Just follow the love*", you're getting all hippy on me today."

"Dad, why are we so obsessed?"

"What do you mean Jess?"

"Well, I mean everything that a Passaro does is so obsessive. I mean you can't even coach a ten year old baseball team without trying to win a national championship, or as soon as the boys start to wrestle you have your sights on winning a State Championship?" Jess says.

"Jess, you call that being obsessive, I call that having a goal and being focused. It is a great characteristic to have, but you have to be careful. There is a fine line between focus and obsession," I say to her.

I add: "Jess there are two things that I know about us Passaro's. That we are fighters, and we know how to win."
My mind emerges from the memory of my last talk with Jess.

*We are fighters and we know how to win.*

*We are fighters and we know how to win.*

I repeat this to myself over and over as I look at Jess in her bed attached to a machine that is breathing for her.

Follow the love, Jess.

*We are fighters and we know how to win.*

# Chapter 6

# Starting to Build a Team

I'm not looking for the best players,

I'm looking for the right one's.


Herb Brooks


When asked why he did not select the most talented players

For his 1980 Olympic Hockey Team.

It couldn't have been more than an hour after BettyJane had left the hospital in almost four days that I picked up my cell phone, walked into the stairwell of the ICU and dialed her number.

"BettyJane, I need for you to come back to the hospital."

There was no conversation afterward, no sound, no good bye, nothing. There was no need for discussion, based on the tone of my voice, there could only be one reason why I would want her to come back so soon.

And it wasn't good.

Twenty minutes later she arrived back at the hospital and I filled her in.

"Jessie's CT scan revealed some serious things that we need to act on immediately, her brain is swelling and they need to relieve the pressure that is building up on it. " I tell her.

"But she looks fine." BettyJane replies.

And in a weird way she is right. Jess looks very peaceful right now.

"They say that unless we reduce the pressure it may accelerate very quickly." I pause for a second. "She is scheduled for brain surgery in the morning."

As we are speaking the nurses come into the room and start to prep Jess for surgery.

There is an argument that breaks out between BettyJane and the nurses. BettyJane will not allow the nurses to cut Jess's hair off. No matter what they say or do, BettyJane just won't budge.

"It's her hair – she loves her hair…it won't be Jess without her hair."

She cries into my shoulder.

I finally come up with a solution.

"What if we leave a long strand of auburn hair in the back of Jess's head, just like Sampson?" I compromisingly ask.

"That would work," I hear from both sides.

The nurses then shave Jess's head and leave a long auburn braided ponytail in the back.

Jess is now bald and looks like a cross between Sinead O'Connor and Sampson.

BettyJane and I both silently ask God to give Jess super human strength just like He did for Sampson.

I ask, but I get no feeling back.

Dr. Leon, who will be performing the operation in the morning, walks into the room and details the process of the operation to BettyJane and I.

"We will take out a piece of her skull, to give the pressure room to release itself. We will then make an incision in her abdomen and keep the piece of her skull there, incubated, until it is time to put it back into her head again," the doctor says to us.

"Her name is Jess, not 'her'", I say rather abruptly.

"I'm very sorry – you are right," Dr. Leon apologetically replies.

"I need to know if you have a Do Not Resuscitate order," he somberly asks. "I will do the best that I can, but sometimes things are out of our control, and I need to know your wishes."

"Doctor, please don't give me the "I'll do the best that I can speech", I need you to fight for Jess. As long as there is a chance I want you to realize my wife's and my stance. I don't care if the chance is 1%; it is up to my wife and myself to get it to 2%, then 4%, then and 8%. That is what as parents we are supposed to do, right?"

I continue: "Doctor, if you were me, what would you do right now?"

"Mr. Passaro, the quality of life...," he starts to say and interrupts himself and changes course.
"I understand, I really do. I will fight for Jess," he says as he departs.

There is something about Dr. Leon that I like. He is able to go from doctor to human instantaneously. He has an empathetic side.

BettyJane and I continue to talk, mostly about Dr. Leon and the feeling that we have about his ability to put himself in our shoes. A nurse overhears our conversation and says: "I don't mean to eavesdrop, but you are right. Dr. Leon just lost his wife recently, he knows exactly how you feel."

It is at this instance that I know I have a very valuable asset, the ability to sense the unknown and trust my feelings.

There is not another doctor in the world that I would want to be performing brain surgery on my daughter tomorrow morning, than Dr. Leon.

If I was the general manager putting together my daughters "team" of people who I want to help Jess recover, I would draft Dr. Leon in the first round.

I don't know if he is the most talented doctor.

But I do know that he is the right one.

# Chapter 7

# Hallway or Private Room

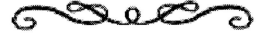

A heart breaking

Isn't always as loud as a bomb exploding...

Sometimes it can be as quiet as a feather falling.

And the most painful thing is

No one really hears it,

Except you.


Unknown

**August 26th, 2009**

I am sitting in the waiting room of the major surgery section of the hospital.

One scene plays out over and over again.

Loved ones would frantically wait for a doctor to peak their head into the waiting room, call them over where they would find out the fate of the rest of their lives.

I am very good in math, and I happen to pick up on patterns very quickly.

I figured out the pattern.

After being in the waiting room for more than four hours I have noticed that when the doctor summons the loved ones to come outside in the hallway to talk, that those loved ones come back with joyful tears.

And when the doctor summons the loved ones to come into another room to talk, that those loved ones come back with sad tears. In those cases the tears are flowing down the loved ones faces and there is usually someone at their side attempting to keep them upright while their knees are bending and buckling as they try to walk out of the room with their shattered lives.

I wonder which one that I will be.

Finally Dr. Leon peaks into the room and summons BettyJane and I outside into the hallway.

He doesn't need to say a word.

Dr. Leon starts to talk doctorease to us: "Things went well, we did the best that we could, only time will tell."

I convert him back into a human by asking him:
"Dr. did you fight for Jess."

"Mr. Passaro, I didn't need to – everything went as best that it could."

"Thank you," I say, as I look him in the eye.

He is telling the truth.  I can see it in his eyes.

"Jess will be in the post op for a few hours, and then you can see her back in the ICU," Dr. Leon says as he sets off for his second brain surgery of the morning.

I am one of the people with joyful tears.

# Chapter 8

# There is an Open Circle

There are 86,400 seconds in a day.

It's up to you to decide what to do with them.

It has been one hundred and eight hours since BettyJane or I have slept. Unless you count sitting upright in a chair, closing your eyes for a few moments and using the wall as a pillow, as sleep.

Mentally I am rejuvenated; physically I am breaking down.
I have a deep chest cold coming on; I fear that it is bronchitis.

BettyJane and I decide that I should get to a doctor to take care of it right away, and stay away until I am fine. That means that she would need to spend the next 48 hours at the hospital by herself. That would take her up to one hundred and fifty six hours straight at the hospital.

I feel horrible that I can't stay, but it is the right move.

I hug BettyJane and I head out back into the world.

My first stop is at Dr. Iwai's office for an antibiotic for myself. He sees me without an appointment and asks me about my wife and my family. I fill him in on the events that have transpired and his face wrinkles in sadness. He has a special relationship with my wife – he just loves her innocence. I see true sadness in his eyes as I leave his office, prescription in hand.

I have this overwhelming feeling that I should be doing more right now, that there has to be something that I could be doing to improve the situation.

I am so tired.

I hear in my head *"There is an open circle."* And my wrestler's mentality takes over.

You see twenty-six years ago, when I was in high school, my goal and mission in life was to win a New York State Wrestling Championship.

I committed myself to a lifestyle, made the sacrifices, put in the time, starved myself, shaved my head, I had the hunger, the desire and the determination, but I came up short.

For many years, after I graduated it seemed like I got nothing out of my six years of total dedication to the sport. That the trade off of what I gave and what I got in return to this sport was way out of whack.

I hated wrestling for it.

To put every ounce of your soul into achieving something and to get nothing out of it in return was beyond my comprehension and I just could not justify it in my head.

Until I had adversity in my life.

And slowly but surely, I started realizing how much the sport of wrestling actually has given back to me. Much more than I ever knew.

When life throws you to your back, you need to know how not to get pinned, get off of your back and do enough to make up the difference in order to win.

*"There is an open circle."* This mantra keeps ringing in my ears.

In order to achieve the results that you want you need to do the things that others are not wiling or able to do.

*"There is an open circle."*

This mantra is what my high school coaches would say to me during wrestling practice when they knew that I was physically exhausted and was about to rest for a moment. There was an open circle on the wrestling mat, and if I was interested I could get out there and do more.

*"There is an open circle."*

Meaning there is still more that you could do.  Don't rest now; this is where the difference is made.  To work when you are mentally and physically exhausted gets you to the next level.

*"There is an open circle."*

When I heard those words back in high school, I would immediately ignore my fatigue and realize that there was still more that I could do.

*"There is an open circle."*

No time for rest.

It is time to get back to work.

# Chapter 9

# Be the Guy Who Sets the Bar.

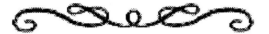

People who say that it cannot be done

Should not interrupt those that are doing it.


George Bernard Shaw

After a few hours of forced sleep, I am on my way to taking Maverick and Travis to wrestling practice.

We arrive at practice. The kids get ready by lacing up their shoes and I find an out of the way spot in the parent's area to sit down and rest.

I must look like hell.

I'm too tired to care what I look like.

I cross my arms across my chest and I close my eyes for a few seconds. It feels like a few hours.

Practice begins.

Mike Patrovich's resounding voice yells out: "Start circling it up."

And on command about twenty wrestlers get on their feet and start jogging around the two steel posts that are on opposite sides of the room.

Practice is intense.

They wrestle for eighty minutes of the scheduled ninety-minute practice when Mike yells out:

*"Hey listen to me.*

*I know you are tired.*

*You got to train your mind and your body when they are tired.*

*This is about toughness, not necessarily about conditioning.*

*Get a little stronger; get a little tougher.*

*No breaks.*

*Don't take a break."*

For the next ten minutes twenty aspiringly elite wrestlers sprint to exhaustion.

After about sixty push ups, they are done and Mike brings them into the middle of the mat to talk to them while they stretch and recover.

This is the best part of practice.

I have always videotaped these talks because they are so valuable. Today is no different.

Mike starts out:

*"There is nothing like a hot summer day to be in a basement wrestling room.*

*It can teach you a lot.*

*The one thing that it could teach you is to push yourself.*

*What I watched happen was that there were a few guys who kind of set the bar and battled when they were tired, which caused a domino affect.*

*I watched the tired guys look over to the group that was working hard and say to themselves: "I can do that."*

*At first they were feeling sorry for themselves, and after looking at the guys who set the bar, the tired wrestlers raised their level.*

**Be the guy who sets the bar.**

*It's not going to kill you.*

*I had a lot of practices where I thought I was going to die.*

*The truth is - It never happened.*

**You can always work harder.**

*Be the guy that sets the bar."*

I am no longer tired.

The bar has been raised.

Wrestling is starting to give back to me at a time when I need it the most.

# Chapter 10

# Awakenings

How kind is it to give life,

Only to take it away?

It's given to and taken away from all of us.

Awakenings

**August 29th, 2009**

It is the first night that I am sleeping in my own bed in over a week.

Alone.

I can't sleep.

I don't want to sleep.

It is after midnight.

I get out of bed and walk down the hallway towards Jess's bedroom.

I step over the area where I remember picking Jess up a week ago, and I enter Jess's bedroom.

I turn on the light.

So many colors.  Each of Jess's walls is painted a different color.

So much expression.  There is freehand art on each of Jess's walls.

So much life.  Pictures are hung up all over the place on corkboards.

So much to fight for.

I turn out the light.

So much has changed.

I head back to my room and I lie down.

I insert earphones into my ears and I hit the playlist on my iTunes.

And for the next two hours I torture myself playing the Evanescence song "Bring Me Back to Life."

*"Wake me up, wake me up inside, I can't wake up.*
*Wake me up inside, save me.*

*Call my name and save me from the dark, wake me up,*
*Bid my blood to run, I can't wake up.*

*Before I become undone, save me.*
*Save me from the nothing I've become.*

*Now that I know what I'm without*
*You can't just leave me*
*Breathe into me and make me real, bring me back to life.*

*I've been sleeping a thousand years it seems.*

*I've got to open my eyes to everything.*

*Don't let me die here.*
*There must be something wrong.*
*Bring me back to life.*
*Wake me up, wake me up inside, I can't wake up.*
*Wake me up inside, save me.*

*Call my name and save me from the dark, wake me up,*
*Bid my blood to run, I can't wake up."*

Over and over again.

Hell is giving an obsessive person a problem that they cannot solve.

Life in a loop.

Over and over again.

As if that is not torture enough, I watch the video.

Over and over again.

I got to stop this torture.

I got to turn this around.

I start googleing success stories of people who successfully emerged from Jess's state.

After some time I come across the 1990 movie "Awakenings", with Robin Williams.

I watch the movie in its entirety in the wee hours of the morning.

The movie "Awakenings" is about an obsessed doctor who believes that patients that have been in a catatonic state for over thirty years due to Encephalitis are alive inside; after he sees a small reaction that one patient has to a stimulus.

Everyone thinks that he is crazy.
Until he wakes up a patient and brings him back to life by giving him L-Dopa.

I search the Internet.

The story is true; the real life doctor is Dr. Oliver Sacks. It happened in 1969.

I may be crazy, but I vaguely remember one doctor asking another doctor the night that this occurred if he did an Encephalitis test, and his answer was "No we didn't have time."

*"Don't let me die here.*
*There must be something wrong.*
*Bring me back to life."*

Over and over again…
There is a fine line between being focused and obsessed.

Sometimes obsession is just what the doctor ordered.

# Chapter 11

# One Person with Belief

# Is Worth a Thousand People

# With Only an Interest

Never doubt

That a small, thoughtful, committed group of people

Can change the world.

It is the only thing that ever has.

When I coached youth baseball, I built teams that had one goal in mind: To win a baseball game in Cooperstown on a Thursday during the summer.

I called the mission "Thursday Baseball."

You see, the Cooperstown Dreams Park Tournament was the best Youth National Baseball Tournament in the country, and the championship game was played on Thursday.

64 teams from all around the country came in every week of the summer to vie for a championship.

For various reasons, a New York team never won a Cooperstown Dreams Park Championship.

I set out to do so.

Over the years I brought eight different teams to Cooperstown.

On each attempt, the teams got closer and closer to playing on Thursday.

It was during these four years that I learned the magical formula for success:

Belief + Team + Hard Work + Passion = Success

I quickly figured out why a New York Team never won.

*They believed the reasons why everyone told them that they couldn't win.*

"How can you compete with California kids when they get to play year round?" the nonbelievers would say.

"Florida kids are just more talented, they have major leaguers coaching them."

"They have been playing together for years, you will never beat them."

The truth is, whatever you really truly believe becomes your reality.

I truly believed that one of the reasons that a New York team never won a Championship at Cooperstown Dreams Park was because they didn't *really* try to win because they didn't believe that they could win.

They believed in the excuses more than they believed in themselves. Don't get me wrong, everyone tries to win, but not everyone is willing to sacrifice so much for such a small chance to win a National Title.

In New York it meant to play a different style of baseball than what was played locally. It meant playing with leading and stealing at an early age, it meant playing on a larger field, it meant valuing the details, the bunting, taking pitches, defense, and the ability to accept your roles. It meant that everyone on the team needed to know how to pitch, hit behind the runners and know how to run the bases.

Most importantly it meant believing in yourself more than believing in the reasons why everyone else felt that you couldn't win.

Each year I set out to build a team of players, who believed, who wanted to be on the team and who had the passion to pursue winning under all adverse conditions.

I simplified the formula to find the right players - the players who believed.

Over time I came up with a simply ingenious way of finding the right players for the team.

My solution was this: I held tryouts at 5:30 am on a Sunday morning in the dead of winter at an indoor facility.

Why 5:30 am on a Sunday morning in February?

It was because if a player truly desired to be there, he could be. No one has anything to do at 5:30 am on a Sunday in February in New York.

The first ninety percent of the tryout was a meaningless mixture of fielding, hitting and pitching drills. This is where everyone thought that they needed to shine in order to make the team.

They couldn't have been further from the truth.

In the last ten percent of the practice I would line the players up in height order and ask them to walk in a single file line around the perimeter of the facility.

Their mission was to walk together with one head directly behind the other head in perfect unison.

They were instructed to only look forward.

Not left.

Not right.

Not back.

Only forward.

I let them know that the players who accomplished this were on the team.

The players, who couldn't, no matter how talented, were not.

I was looking for one head, with 10 hearts and one beat.

That was my team.

You see, I could teach a kid to hit, to throw or to run the bases, but I couldn't teach him to believe.

So as time went by, one by one I accumulated players who believed.

My players were never the most imposing looking athletes.

You never saw fear in the eyes of opposing teams as we approached the field for a game.

But you did see disbelief in their eyes as we walked off of the field after the game.

You could almost always hear them muttering to themselves: "How did that team just run rule us?"

I always laughed when I heard that.

The truth is, I could have given every opposing team the formula before the season and it still wouldn't have mattered.

It was too simple.


Simple enough to do, but just as simple not to do.

My answer to myself was always:
"You just don't get it. When a team works together for a common cause that they are passionate about, it is not about your height, or your weight, it is about your belief and your heart."

No one valued belief more than I did.

I truly had a great feeling in my heart, when most of the players on my team went on and won a Championship at Cooperstown Dreams Park while playing for another New York team. Even though there was a falling out among parents, and they achieved this goal on another team, I was just very happy to add the most crucial ingredient to their success.

Belief.

**August 31st, 2009**

For the last two days I have been receiving reports back from BettyJane about Jess's progress after her brain surgery.

When Jess came back to the room after the operation, and after being weaned off of the Propofol, Jess's eyes opened.

No dramatic opening and rebirth, but a slight, very tired, opening of her eyelids.

BettyJane and I adjusted our shifts to include an overlap of time when we could both be together for an hour after each of our shifts, to update each other on the day's occurrences, just so we were both on the same page of what was happening.

During our first overlap update, BettyJane fills me in that she saw Jess open her eyes and move a little.

I am real excited.

She is distraught.

"Why are you so sad? This is a good thing", I tell her.

"No, its not – they said to me 'Don't read into this, it doesn't mean anything'."

She went on.

"And after I noticed Jess moving ever so slightly they told me 'That was a reflexive reaction, she is not moving voluntarily'."

"They said that parents see what they want to see, that they just don't want to see reality."

I am fuming.
At the same time BettyJane is updating me on the days events, a doctor walks in, goes to Jess's bed, reads her chart and says:

"No change – no brain activity."

I immediately say, "Who are you?"

"I am Dr. Soandso, I am filling in for Dr. Leon who is on another shift."

"Can I speak with you outside, doctor?

"Right after my rounds", he dismisses me.

"No – NOW", I assert.

When we get outside I say: "Don't you ever speak in front of my daughter like she is not there, do you hear me?"

"If you would like to speak to me, you speak to me outside," I continue.

"Mr. Passaro, you and your wife have to realize that you are seeing things that as a parent you want to see. She is not moving. I don't want to give you false hope." He bluntly states.

"Doctor, It seems to me that while everyone is so busy making sure that they don't give my wife and myself false hope, they are forgetting to realize that in the process they are eliminating all hope."

"Mr. Passaro, medically speaking…," he starts to say as I cut him off.

"You're not God, you don't get to determine who is going to make it or not. Your job is to get your patients to make it, you are on the team of trying to make them make it."

"Mr. Passaro, you have to realize the odds," he says.

"Let me ask you one question doctor. Do you believe that Jess will make it?" I put him on the spot.

He does not respond.

"Doctor, your services are no longer needed," I say and I walk back into my daughters ICU room.

"Mr. Passaro, can I meet with you and your wife in my office?"
An official looking woman asks me a few hours later.

BettyJane and I oblige.

"Mr. Passaro you can't tell doctors that their services are no longer needed," she starts the conversation.

"Yes I can, I did, and I will continue to do so."

"Why did you do that?" she asks.

"Because he doesn't believe." I reply.

"It isn't his job to believe," she replies.

"Well that is where you are wrong," I say. "If he is on my team he needs to believe."

"And what about the nurse you dismissed from her services earlier today," she brings up.

"She talked like Jess was not there. She didn't believe either," I informed her.

"Mr. Passaro, you can't dismiss everyone who doesn't believe in your daughters recovery. We have a set of rules that we follow, shifts, and rotations. I can't rearrange everything for you to only have believers," she says to me, sounding very annoyed.

"Yes you can, but it's not important enough for you to do so. But it is important enough for me to build a medical team of believers, and I will continue to do so. So anyone who talks in front of Jess as if she is not there, or refers to her as a "her", or doesn't want to get emotionally attached will not be on Jess's team," I emphatically inform her.

"You may only have a few people, Mr. Passaro," she says in a solemn tone.

"That is fine, I just need the ones that believe."

One person with belief is worth a thousand people with only an interest.

*One head.*
*Ten hearts.*
*One beat.*

I walk back into my room; I am followed in by another doctor who says to me:

"Mr. Passaro, let me teach you about how medicine works," he starts out.

"One of two things is going to happen. Either the doctors are going to say I told you so, or they are going to say that Jess was the exception. What *you believe* will determine who gets to say I told you so to whom."

"Never stop believing," he begs me.

"Doctor, you are on the team." I say.

He smiles.

# Chapter 12

# Zihuatenejo

Amazing Awaits


When you work hard enough,

Want badly enough,

And refuse to say:

"I've had enough."


Amazing Awaits

**September 1st, 2009**

An avalanche in your head.

That is how a brain injury is described on one of the posts that I am reading on the Internet at 2:48 am.

I know that Jess is in there.

I have seen slight movements.  Real movements.

I can't imagine being Jess right now.

I don't want to imagine being Jess right now.

I have to imagine being Jess right now.

An avalanche in your head.

What would I do?

What does she need?

Hope.

I immediately take out my iPhone and go to YouTube and I search for videos from the Shawshank Redemption.

I pull up a video of the conversation that Andy Dufrense and Red are having in the courtyard of the prison, about hope.

Andy asks Red: "Where are you going to go when you get out of here?"

Red responds sarcastically: "One day when I have a long white beard and two or three marbles left, maybe they will let me out of here."

Andy, with a dream in his eye immediately cuts him off and says: "I'll tell you where I would go – Zihuatenejo.  It's in Mexico, a little place on the Pacific Ocean… Open up a little hotel, right on the beach, buy some worthless boat and fix it up like new and take my guests out charter fishing."

Red shoots Andy down and says: "I don't think you should be doing this to yourself, Andy.  Mexico is way the hell down there, and you are in here and that is just the way it is."

Andy defiantly responds: "I guess that it comes down to one simple choice really – Get busy living, or get busy dying."

An avalanche in your head.

Get busy living, or get busy dying.

It took Andy Dufrense twenty years to chip away at his prison wall and escape from his hell.

Hope is what kept his dream alive.

It is time to start moving the rocks away from Jess's brain avalanche so she can escape to her Zihuatenejo.

It is now 3:03 am and I approach Jess's bed and I whisper in her ear: "Jess, I believe that you are in there. I am here to get you out. We need to get other people to believe also. So what I want you to do is to move something, other than your hands, because they think that your hand movement is not voluntary. I need you to concentrate on putting your two big toes together."

"Jess, I want you to imagine that you are laying on the beach in the Hamptons right now…"

I sit back down and start to coach Jess.

Jess's legs are separated by at least two feet in length at this point.

"Come on Jess, you can do this…"

"Come on Jess, you can do this…"

"Prove to everyone that you are in there."

Over and over again.

When you stare at something for twenty minutes straight sometimes your mind plays games on you and makes it look like there is movement, when there really is not.

I try to play devils advocate and dismiss the slight movement that I think I see to the above phenomenon.

But it is undeniable.

Jess's legs are getting closer and closer together.
"Come on Jess, you can do this!" my voice is crescendoing.

It is now nearly forty minutes since I started coaching Jess to touch her two big toes together.

Her two feet are now about one foot apart.

"Come on Jess, come on Jess, come on Jess."

My coaching is non-stop at this point and my excitement is almost at a feverish pitch and nearly uncontrollable.

I look up from Jess's legs and I see the head nurse approaching her room.

I am so excited that I am crying at this point. I feel the warmest tear roll down my cheek. It hits my mouth. I can taste the salt.

The head nurse enters the room. I immediately explain to her what has happened and she says to me: "Mr. Passaro, you need to keep it down in here before you wake up the other patients."

"Nurse, my daughter, on command has moved her feet about a foot over the last forty minutes, I am a little excited – try to understand…," I say.

I beg her to watch for a few minutes. She watches for thirty seconds and says, "I don't see anything, and I need to get back to the desk.

Please keep your voice down or I am going to have to ask you to leave."

Nothing is going to derail me so I play the game and say: "Of course."

Over the next twenty minutes, Jess has cut the distance between her big toes down to about six inches.

Then four inches.

Then two inches.

I can't believe what I am seeing.

Actually I can believe it. I knew she was in there.

Jess is trembling now trying to get her toes to come together for the last inch. She is battling, it is not enough to her that she moved her legs together almost two feet over the last ninety minutes – it seems like the last inch is most important to her.

It has been another forty minutes and her two big toes are within a hair of each other.

"One big push Jess."

"One big one Jess."

I ask her to give it everything that she has for one big push to get her toes together.

It is the most beautiful site that I have ever seen in my life.

Jess's toes jump together.

I hug her.

Zihuatenejo.

Get busy living or get busy dying.

# Chapter 13

# Deadly Premonition

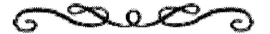

Be careful what you ask for,

Sometimes it is exactly what you get.

**September 12th, 2009**

The Super 32 wrestling tournament, held in North Carolina in late October, is the most competitive preseason high school wrestling tournament in the country.

Virtually every quality wrestler in the country makes the trip to Greensboro to prove their mettle.

There are over 160+ wrestlers per weight class and placing (1-8) in this tournament has always been followed with a deluge of attention from most every Division 1 college coach in existence.

This tournament has been on our event calendar for over a year.

It is six weeks away.

In order to attend this event, a major commitment will be needed from both Maverick and Travis and from my wife and myself.

Registration for the tournament opens up online in five minutes. Last year the 2,500 wrestler capacity tournament sold out in only eight minutes.

There is no time to think…

Every rational bone in my body it telling me not to go.

I register the boys for the tournament.

Before I can doubt my decision I immediately book and pay for airplane tickets and a hotel for the event for the three of us, on Expedia.

There is no turning back now.

We are going.

I want both.

I look at the calendar and I plan out the weekends for the next six weeks. In order to get the boys in shape for the tournament it will require four of our next six weekends to be on the road traveling to out of state wrestling tournaments.

On its own, this schedule would be a major commitment and intense part of the wrestling season. Under the current circumstances, it may require an insane man to pull it off.

I fit the bill as a psycho, so it may work.

I vow that only death will stop us from attending the Super 32.

# Chapter 14

# One Step Forward, Two Steps Back

Sometimes the questions are complicated

And the answers are simple.

Dr. Seuss

It is amazing; everyday some very smart people give Jess a neurological exam at 6:00 am and conclude that she is nonresponsive.

The right conclusion is that she is nonresponsive at 6:00 am.

If they gave Jess this same exam when she was healthy at 6:00 am, they would have come up with the same conclusion:
Non-Responsive.

It is amazing that smart people keep the variables of the experiment the same everyday, and think that they are seeing the full picture.

If BettyJane and I weren't here with Jess twenty-four hours per day and we had to rely on their "updates" of Jess's condition I would almost believe them that Jess was not moving and is non responsive.

They could be so convincing.

I keep telling the neurologists that if they want to see Jess move they need to come to her room between 6:00 pm and 9:00 pm. I don't know why, but Jess moves a great deal during those hours.

Doctor after doctor gave me the same response: "Your daughter is not my only patient. My rounds will not allow me to come to her room during those hours."

And my response to them is always the same: "Jess *is* my only patient and your services are no longer needed."

Dr. Leon listened and visited Jess today around 7:00 pm. He witnessed Jess moving like we have been saying she has been. He also said that Jessie's CT Scan is getting better and better; that it is not like anything that he has ever seen. He believes now that Jess does not have a full brain injury – that every brain injury is different and he believes that Jess is improving each day.

He added that BettyJane and I as parents did the right thing by never stop believing. He said that he has never seen a case like this before. He added that most patients that lose oxygen to their brains for the time that Jess lost it to her brain never really move or improve at all.

Dr. Leon's body language is very positive.

I am very encouraged by his visit. I am glad to have him on our team.

That is the good news.

The bad news is that that right after Dr. Leon left the room another doctor entered and said that after fourteen days it is routine for a patient on a breathing tube to get a tracheostomy. He explained that a tracheostomy is a surgical procedure that will create an opening in Jess's neck where a tube will be inserted into her windpipe. This will provide an airway for her to breath and will allow us to remove secretions from her lungs with a drawing tube.

Jess is scheduled for the procedure immediately.

She also needs a procedure to move her feeding tube from her mouth to her stomach.

Jess is back from the procedures.

I don't know if I would rather have all the tubes away from her face or not.

Without them, there is the stark reality that this really is Jess lying here and it is much harder to look at her.

Jess's eyes are swollen and are black and blue.

How did we get here? This can't really be happening.

I notice that a piece of Jess's tongue is missing. I am told that Jess bit down and would not unclench her grip for over twenty minutes and unfortunately bit off a part of her tongue.

I am hit with a wave of emotion as I think back to Percy from "The World According to Garp." I recall that your tongue does not grow back and it is needed to speak.

I hope that Jess still has enough of her tongue left to speak.

I cry.

I know the answer to improving Jess's condition doesn't lay with tears, that the answer is in sweat.

I need to acquire the knowledge to beat each one of Jess's disabilities.

I need to learn how the brain works so I can send commands to her body parts and teach her how to swallow again, how to think again, how to communicate again and how to love again.

That is the big one - to love again.

Without love there is no life.

As long as Jess will be able to love again, I will fight forever.

The journey to find and learn all of the specializations needed to get Jess to her maximum capability started the second her two toes touched a few days ago.

My plan is to take each disability and attack it like a Rick Pitino full court press.

To create small achievable goals that when accumulated will add up to the ultimate goal.

I believe that everything that I have experienced in my life was to prepare me to SAVE my daughter's life.

I look into Jess's eyes. Something does not seem right. Her eyes are slightly bloodshot and she seems to be distant.

My hope is that the slight, easily overlooked and dismissed signs of slight blood shot eyes, extended sleep patterns, a very slight fever and throbbing in her left temple are not all connected. All of these would never be picked up by anyone who did not spend most of the day with Jess. By themselves they are nothing, hopefully they are not all related.

I prepare myself for the worst.

# Chapter 15

# Blind or Deaf?

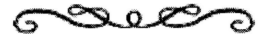

Is there anything worse than being blind?

Yes, a man with sight and no vision.

Helen Keller

The infectious disease doctor is talking to me and I am in a daze.

"Mr. Passaro – what should we do?"

It is as if Charlie Brown's teacher is talking to me – I can see his lips moving, but all I hear is "Blah Blah Blah Blah Bah."

My mind is reviewing the night's events. My instinct was right. Last night at about 2:00 am Jess spiked a fever to over 103 degrees. With every degree of temperature above the norm, ones heart rate will increase ten beats per minute more than usual. Jess's heart rate went from 85 beats per minute to a sustained 135 beats per minute.

Danger land.

Jess also vomited. To see a helpless person who cannot move throw up is one of the most chilling to the core events that you will ever see in your life.

It nearly broke me.

I am just glad that I was there to help her because Jess could have choked on her own vomit and died.

"How much can I take?" I ask myself and immediately respond back to myself: "I can take as much as they can dish out. Bring it on."

After I helped Jess get past the vomiting, Jess just endlessly stared into space. This is almost a sure sign of aspiration, Jess swallowing some of her own vomit, which almost always leads to pneumonia.

As I slowly drift back into reality the doctor explains to me that Jess has two very dangerous types of super bugs, one colonized in her chest and the other one in her head.

A super bug infection is a bacterium that gets stronger when it mutates to beat the antibiotics given to destroy it, thus making it resistant to almost all treatments.

The infectious disease doctor is telling me that they had to let Jess's infection turn into pneumonia so they would have a better chance to treat it.

I don't understand the strategy, but that is beside the point because I am being told that Jess now has klebsiella pneumonia, a very dangerous form of pneumonia that is highly lethal.

Charlie Browns teacher is back.

I don't know how long I am gone but eventually I come back too.

"Mr. Passaro, there are only two antibiotics left that can potentially beat these superbugs: Amakacin and Polymixin. They are both very toxic with potentially major side affects. One sometimes causes blindness and the other sometimes causes deafness. Which one would you prefer we use?"

Did he just ask me whether I prefer Jess to be blind or deaf?

"Doctor, are you 100% sure that those are the only two options?" I ask as a last resort.

"Actually we won't have the lab results back until the morning, but it may be too late at that time," the doctor informs me.

"What do you mean too late?"

He does not reply and puts his head down for a second.

"Here is what we are going to do – we are going to tell the lab to expedite the blood work. How long will that take?"

"We can probably get the results in a few hours," he says.

"Ok, let's wait on the results then," I direct him.

After a few hours of pure torture waiting on the results, the results bring good news. Jess's infection is Acinetobacter, which can be treated with the antibiotic Roceplin. This bacterium has not built up a resistance to this antibiotic as of yet.

I can't believe I have to make these life saving decisions on virtually no sleep and when I am most vulnerable myself.

I cannot believe what has happened over the last twenty-four hours.

I am just glad that I will be picking the boys up in the morning to go to Stamford Connecticut for a wrestling tournament.

I am glad that my decisions will go from choosing being blind or deaf to choosing top, bottom or neutral.

I just can't believe that this is happening.

# Chapter 16

# Fish Hooked – Don't Take the Bait.

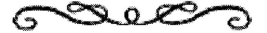

Daniel: You train to fight?

Mr. Miyagi: That what you think?

Daniel: No.

Mr. Miyagi: Then why train?

Daniel: So I won't have to fight.

Mr. Miyagi: Miyagi have hope for you.

The Karate Kid

**September 13th, 2009**

I am sitting on the bleachers in a high school gym some two hundred miles away from Jess's hospital room.

My body is in Connecticut, my mind and heart are in New York. I spend the next forty-five minutes trying to merge the three of them together.

*"If you chase two rabbits, both will escape."*

I keep repeating the lesson that I learned when I was faced with coaching both of my son's baseball teams at the same time in a baseball tournament a few years ago. Both teams had made it into the championship game and the championship games were being played at the same time, in different parts of the complex.

My solution was to run back and forth to each game as much as I could, exactly like Greg Brady did in the episode of "The Brady Bunch" when he was seeing two girls at the same time.

I got the same result as he did by doing so.

As much as I tried, no matter where I physically was, my mind was at the other game. It was a rookie mistake and one that disallowed me from being of any help to either team.

*"If you chase two rabbits, both will escape."*

I pledge to myself that while I am in Connecticut with the boys at a wrestling tournament that my body, my mind and my heart will all be here also.

One rabbit at a time I can handle.

I focus on my new anxiety – In every wrestling match, somewhere during the match, one wrestler will realize that he will not be able to win and he will break. It happens in every match, at different points during the match, but it happens. And when it does it is the most obvious thing to the experienced eye.
Am I pushing the boys too much, to soon to compete?

How will they handle the challenge of fight or flight?

Will they be able to harness their built up frustration and anger or will they explode and cause a scene that no one will understand?

I hope I am doing the right thing.

There is a fine line between tough and crazy, and I know that I am flirting with it.

Over the course of the next six hours both Maverick and Travis show signs of really developing as wrestlers. Their stance, their offense, their defense and their desire are all at a noticeably higher level.

I am amazed that they are able to stay strong and perform.

Maverick won three of the four matches that he wrestled. His only loss came at the hands of a wrestler from upstate.
In that match, a call did not go Mavericks way, and instead of getting two points for a takedown, the teenage referee decided to give Maverick's opponent the takedown after a scramble and two very quick back points. Maverick handled it very well, he fought to the end and he very impressively kept his cool.

He has come a long way, as probably six months ago we would have had a much different mental showing during the match when the call did not go his way.

Travis's day was a little bizarre, and quite honestly, a very cruel test.

Travis also technically won three of his four matches. In the match that Travis "lost" he was totally dominating the match. The score was 14-0 in the second period. (Once a wrestler goes up by 15 points they stop the match and award the wrestler with a win by technical fall). Travis needed to score one more point to get the tech.

As they were wrestling, the two wrestlers went out of bounds.

And then a scene right out of the "Karate Kid" breaks out, the one where the evil coach gives the command to "Sweep the Leg."

As the two wrestlers were walking back to the center of the circle to finish the match, the coach gets the attention of his wrestler and gives him a command. The coach takes his forefinger and inserts it into his mouth and pulls on his own cheek. The communication was blatant and obvious.

Up 14-0, Travis is on the top position to restart the match. The whistle blows; Travis's opponent immediately reaches back, inserts his fingers into Travis's mouth and wrenches his neck around. Travis and everyone mat side are pleading to the teenage referee that the kid has his hands in Travis's mouth, Travis is actually bleeding from his mouth. The referee ignores the pleas as Travis is yanked to his back, choked and quick pinned.

Now the evil Sensei coach rushes the mat, picks up his wrestler in jubilation all within the punching distance of Travis.

"Don't do it Trav, don't do it Trav!" I say helplessly to myself.

After Travis provides proof of the fishhook by showing the ref his scratched bloody mouth, the referee adds fuel to the fire by making Travis come back into the circle to shake hands the right way. Thus giving Travis another opportunity to explode.

He doesn't.

Although he was fish hooked, he didn't take the bait.

During the three-hour trip back home, I realize that my mind has been concentrating on something other than life or death.

Mission accomplished.

Time to get back to Jess.

# Chapter 17

# Bob

Death is no more

Than passing from one room

Into another.

Helen Keller

**September 14th, 2009**

At 9:00 am, on September 11th, 2001 my father was scheduled to have his right leg amputated due to complications from diabetes.
As you could imagine, he never did have the operation that day as every doctor and surgeon was called into New York to help save lives.

As the world was in chaos, my father got to keep his leg for one more week.

Wheelchair bound for the last eight years, my dad has spent six hours a day, every other day at dialysis getting his blood decontaminated.

His dialysis nurse is Mary.

Mary has a son who was in a severe car crash a few months ago and fell into a coma.

Jess is in the same room that Mary's son occupied when he was in the ICU at this hospital.

Next door to Jess is a ninety four year old lady whose daughter has spent every hour with her, but knows the inevitability of her mother's fate. The daughter has been extremely nice to me and Jess and has popped her head into our room at just the right time with two cups of coffee in hand, and a smile on her face.

In ICU room number 3, is an elderly man who has brain cancer. He has a white bandage wrapped around his head, from a recent surgery and has had a deluge of visitors recently.

I will call him Bob.

In room number 4 is a mid twenties male handcuffed to his bed. I'm not sure what he did, or what has happened to him, as he has not had any visitors.

It is 2:00 am in the morning.

Bob is crying.

He is struggling to say something.
I can only hear muffled, incoherent rambles.

For the first time in my life I know something deep down that is absolutely true – Bobs loved ones visited him for the last time yesterday.

They don't know it yet, but I do.

At 7:30 am, the nurses change shifts. Before one shift goes home and the other takes over they bring one another up to date on each patient. They ask that I leave during that half hour period, as they feel if overheard a patient's status report that it would be an invasion of privacy to that patient.

At 8:00 am I reenter the ICU and see the hospital workers mopping room number 3.

Bob is gone.

# Chapter 18

# Day 28

# Eerily Parallel Lives

There are winds of destiny that blow

When we least expect them.

Sometimes they gust with the fury

Of a hurricane,

Sometimes they barely fan one's cheek.


Nicholas Sparks

Message in a Bottle

**September 19th, 2009**

Ever since Jess touched her two toes together a few days ago, Jess has been moving more and more.  She has been moving her hands, opening and shutting her eyes, and moving her head back and forth.

Her favorite movement is touching her toes together.
The process still takes about two hours for her to completely bring them together.

I felt so bad for her the other day, as Jess was ninety minutes into the process, having moved her toes within inches of each other and up walks an unknowing nurse and separates Jess's feet before I could stop her. She felt that Jess looked uncomfortable with her feet so close together.

She had to start all over again. The anguish on her face was heartbreaking.

Today, something triggered when Jess woke up – her eyes looked so alive and she seemed to have more control of the different parts of her body than she ever has had over the last twenty-eight days.

Today Jess seems alive.

It was weird, there was a Code 64 (cardiac arrest) in the ICU this morning and all the nurses started scrambling around, and after a few minutes I could see the look on Jess's face express her feelings:

"This is not for me! The bells and whistles and chaos are not for me – I am ok."

In my daily text message that I send out to my family and close fiends I let everyone know that Jess seems to have more confidence in her eyes and in her look, as if she is saying, "Let's start moving this process along."

These text messages have been a cathartic release for me.

It is 6:00 am and Jess is given her daily neuro exam, which the doctor informs me that there is no change – Jess is still non responsive.

I laugh as he leaves the room.

A few minutes later another doctor walks in and explains to me the procedure that they want Jess to have today.

He is very empathetic and explains the procedure in great detail. They want to insert a filter in Jess's lower half of her body because they found a blood clot in her arms.

I try not to be cynical as I ask:
"Wouldn't it be more important to put the filter in the area that you already know the blood clot exists, rather in a place where you are afraid one may appear?"

It has been my experience in life that when someone lays out a plan that you can poke a hole through, and that plan is implemented anyway, that there was some detail that was omitted along the way.

Now my gut is telling me that in this case the detail is no big deal and that this is a preventative measure, but it just illuminates how one must make decisions not having all of the information.

Doctors don't give you all the details, just the ones that will help you make the decisions that they want you to make.

It is amazing that my decisions are made more on my read on whether I trust, believe and have confidence in the doctor, or not.

In this case, even though I feel that I am not being given all the information, I agree to the procedure. I make a note to never be a puppet, to gather all the information myself from now on.

As the doctor leaves the room with the waiver signed for Jess's procedure, a text message dings on my iPhone:

*"Fight a good fight… I am always thinking of you guys… Today is going to be a great day - The day will get even better…See you this afternoon."*

It is from BettyJanes best friend Terri Gili.

Terri, and her husband Rich, have almost identical and parallel lives as BettyJane and I.

Rich and Terri have four active boys.

Our boys have been teammates on nearly every baseball team that we ever played on, and our children have very similar competitive personalities.

Our lives have run parallel for years now.

Our family's friendship has grown over the years to the point that we both consider each other family.

There are only a few people in the world that you would do anything for, no questions asked, at a seconds notice. The Gili's have been in this category with my family for a while now.

I text Terri back, thank her for her optimism and let her know that I will see her when she gets here later in the day.

A half of a day goes by, and just as I am switching shifts with BettyJane, Terri visits Jess as she has everyday since this ordeal began.

Terri mentions that she is not going to visit too long because she is trying to get rid of a headache.

I kiss BettyJane goodbye, walk towards the door, and I look back at BettyJane and Terri both holding Jess's hands bedside.

Day 28 is over.

But the parallel is just beginning.

# Chapter 19

# The Great Sadness Begins

Sad are only those who understand.


Arab Proverb

On my way home from the hospital, I wonder if Jess has recovered enough to be considered a success – one of the ones who recover enough within the first 28 days to fully recover, the way that the statistics talk about.

After stopping off for a bite to eat, I realize that I need to get to a place where I feel good, a place that I can just relax and be myself.

My car pulls into the parking lot of Baseball Heaven.

I am at home watching youth baseball.

In my past life, coaching youth baseball was my passion and obsession.  One of the two or three places in the world that I feel most at home is on a baseball field.

I have coached in over 1,000 games over the last six years and just sitting and watching a game right now will take my mind off of fixating that today is day number 28.

As I am walking into the complex, through the gates towards the fields, my phone rings.

It is Rich.

And he is crying. I can hardly hear him.

Immediately I think that something bad has happened to Jess.

It has not.

It is Terri.

He informs me that Terri has been rushed to Central Suffolk Hospital in Riverhead.

She has a brain aneurysm.

They need to operate immediately.

I stop paralyzed in my tracks for a second, and then I immediately head over to Central Suffolk Hospital.

I arrive just in time to console Rich and his boys right before they transport Terri to Stony Brook Hospital, where they say that they are better equipped to handle what has happened.

During the forty-five minute ride I wonder if I should call BettyJane and let her know.

I don't know how much more that she can handle.

She deserves to know – it is her best friend.

I decide that it would be best to let her know when there are other people around, so she won't be alone.

I call and inform her of what has happened.

"She was just here."
"She was just here"

BettyJane repeats over and over again.

After a long silence and a brief discussion, BettyJane feels that it is best that I go to Stony Brook University Hospital and that she stay with Jess. I am to keep her updated on everything.

I arrive at the hospital and see Rich and his boys outside the Emergency Room exit.

I wish there was a way that I could absorb their pain.

I would.

I would take it all on myself.

I approach them.

In front of me are five strong men who are visibly shaken to their core.

I am usually not very good at offering my sympathy to others in times of need, but this time I am.

We all hug for a few minutes, wipe away our tears and start to regroup.

After a while we head upstairs to the waiting area and we wait. And we wait, and we wait.

Finally after many hours the doctor comes out and allows the family to visit with Terri.

After another hour Rich asks me to come into Terri's room to visit.

I enter.

I can't believe my eyes.

Terri is on a life support machine, just like the one Jess was on a few days ago.

Less than a day ago Terri was bedside, holding Jess's hand.

Now I am at her bedside, holding her hand.

The Great Sadness has just begun.

# Chapter 20

# Two Roses

Some say love,

It is a razor

That leaves your soul to bleed.


Bette Midler

The Rose

**October 2nd, 2009**

It is the first time in forty-one days that BettyJane and I are together, in the same place, outside of Jess's hospital room.

It is cold, the breeze is blowing significantly and it is lightly drizzling outside.

BettyJane and I are both holding a single rose in our right hand.

"Keep moving forward." I say to myself.

"Not left. Not right."

"Not back."

"But Forward."

Believe it or not, I am forty-four years old and I have never been to a cemetery after a funeral before in my life.

One by one, Terri's friends approach her coffin and they drop their rose onto her casket as they say their goodbyes.

Terri's immediate family and best of friends are near the end of the line.

As the front of the line is steadily approaching the grave, the back of the line refuses to move, somehow hoping that if they don't move forward that what is supposed to happen in the next ten minutes will not actually happen.

It is all too final.

"Keep moving forward."

Across the cemetery I can see the people who have already placed their rose, said their good byes and have headed back to their cars.

The back of the line still refuses to move forward.

A gentlemen in a black suit, whom I don't recognize starts taking each person by the hand, and kindly leads and instructs each loved one to place their rose on the grave site.

The last rose finally has been placed.

How do you leave?

Where do you go?

How do you go on?

"Keep moving forward." I keep repeating to myself.

"Keep moving forward."

My thoughts and love are with the Gili family, but I can't help thinking that in the last thirty-three days my wife has lost two of the most important people in her life.

I think to myself that the next thirty-three days have to be better.

I am dead wrong.

# Chapter 21

# How Cruel Can Life Be?

Coincidence is God's way of remaining anonymous.


Albert Einstein

**October 4th, 2009**

My wife and my father have a great relationship. I could never win an argument with my wife if my father was in ears distance, even if she was dead wrong.

His love for her is obvious.

He is hurting that he is not able to visit Jess in the hospital due to his compromised immune system and his being in a wheel chair.

He is hurting even more knowing that BettyJane is hurting so deeply right now, and there is very little that he can do to comfort her.

So earlier in the day I sent a text out to him and my mom just bringing them up to date with my life's events and how BettyJane was holding up.

I just got a ding on my phone and a text appeared:
*"Please stop texting me – I am not your dad."*

That's strange, so I text back: *"What do you mean you're not my dad, lol?"*

Ding – *"I don't know who you are, I would appreciate if you stop texting me, I just lost my father last week."*

I look down at the number that I text, and I realize that it is off by one digit, so I text back: *"I am truly sorry for your loss – wrong number, my mistake."*

An immediate ding comes back: *"Cherish your days with your dad."*

I sit there and stare at the screen of my phone for what seems like an hour and I brace myself for what is to come…

# Chapter 22

# Tourette's Without Talking

Don't let what you cannot do
Interfere with what you can.

John Wooden

Life is a choice.

I choose to be better rather than bitter.

I choose to be glad rather than sad.

To be thankful, rather than say "Why me?"

Because when it comes down to it, you can find happiness in any and all situations.

It is your choice.

Life really is wonderful. Hard, but amazing.

Sometimes, a lot of times, life doesn't follow the script that we would have written ourselves, had we had the chance.

Sometimes life seems incomplete because, at that moment we haven't seen the whole picture as of yet.

When you live life with belief, confidence and enthusiasm there are really some great moments.

Today I experienced one of those moments.

It has just dawned on me that they have had Jess sedated with Propofol or Morphine since she has been here. My idea was to wean her off of the sedation and to see what would happen.

The doctors agree to my experiment and lower Jess's dosage of medicine a little at a time until she is no longer on any kind of sedation.

After a little while, Jess looks more natural and she moves and follows commands to move her hands.

She has a very mad facial expression and seems to be in pain.

I urge the nurse to let the experiment play out. She obliges.

Jess starts to move her left arm up and she got it all the way up to her head where she tried to rip out one of the electronic monitors. While she was doing so she looked like she was exerting every ounce of energy that she had. She went through multiple facial expressions ranging from sheer determination, to anguish, to disgust, to exhaustion.

After Jess rests a bit, the nurse in the room gets excited and starts giving Jess one command after another without giving Jess any time to respond to her prior command.

She says: "Jess, move your finger."

One second later she says: "Jess, move your hands."

Then she impatiently blurts out: "Move your legs."

I explain to her that she needs to slow down and give Jess time to respond to her command, and that it takes about a minute for her to execute the command.

At this time Jess has her hand in the air, with an open palm.

The nurse says: "Jess move one finger."

After about two minutes the nurse starts to loose patience.

As she turns and walks away I start hysterically laughing.

The nurse turns and says – "What is so funny?"

I nod over to Jess, where Jess has not moved one finger, but has moved four fingers and has left one standing straight up in the air.

I die laughing…

Jess just gave the nurse the finger.

I knew that she was in there.

# Chapter 23

# 6 Beds – 7 Patients – 0 Patience

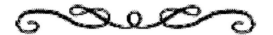

Judge your success

By what you had to give up

In order to get it.


Dalai Lama

**October 5th, 2009**

I cry everyday.

No matter where I am, or what I am doing I cannot stop it from coming on.

At first I can feel the tears start forming on the outside of my eyelids, which I can hold back.

Then my jaw starts to tremor and my top lip starts to quiver and this is where I start to lose control of being in control.

Once my top lip starts to quiver it feels as if the tears are being drawn from all parts of my head around my eyes as the tears are released drowning my eyes.

At this point I must either turn my back to everyone or find a reason to leave the room.

I am currently in the process of looking away to camouflage this occurrence, when I hear BettyJane call me:

"John, before I leave, what do you want to do about parent teachers conferences?"

I don't turn around.

She asks again.

I still don't turn around.

She picks up on what is happening and gives me time.

She understands, because it happens to her too.

Just like a great see saw partner, she realizes that I am down and she transfers some energy to me.

The goal is to have us both on equal terms of energy.

We can never both be down at the same time.

I haven't told her yet.

Jessica is being moved out of the ICU into a step down unit at the hospital.

One might think that I should be ecstatic about this news, that is means that she is improving.

I am not.

All that it means is that there are 7 ICU patients with 6 beds, and Jess is the least acute.

Bottom line, Jess became the least critical in the critical care unit and they needed a bed for someone else.

The ironic part is the success that Jess has been seeing lately will actually be the reason she regresses.

Now Jess will have a roommate and will get less attention and have fewer resources available to her to continue the improvement that she has been making.

Jess will go from having one nurse per patient, to having four patients per nurse.

Now BettyJane is down.

I transfer energy back to her.

By the time I arrive back at the hospital some twelve hours later, Jess is in the step down unit, and she has her worst night in three weeks. Her blood pressure skyrocketed to 150/100 her Resp went to 40 (20 is normal) and her heart rate rose to 155 bpm.

I know that these numbers may not make sense, but they are bad.

It took us five weeks to get Jess stabilized, and it took them one bad decision to cause her chaos again.

The snowball just kept picking up speed downhill all night until finally they had to sedate Jess to get her vitals down.

Hospitals make bad decisions due to a lack of rooms and understaffing and then rationalize it to you as if you can't see right through them.

There should be a 1:1 ratio between patient and nurse and doctor. No changing shifts, no rotations so nurses don't get emotionally attached, no partners of doctors filling in over the weekends or the holidays. If sickness doesn't recognize the weekend or the holiday or emotions why does the care for sickness recognize them?
It is sort of like saying that the cops can't use automatic weapons against the bad guys, but the bad guys can.

It doesn't make sense, because they are trying to make dollars.

Their formula for success is all wrong. The first thing that they should do is to burn all the boats, so retreat is not an option. No option other than the desired result.

Doctors should get paid based on their success rate of curing the patient verse the odds of curing the patient.

Get them so emotionally involved that they become obsessed with getting the patient better.

Oh, that is a family members role instead.

I am sorry if I am sarcastically ranting. I just get so frustrated when things are done for the wrong reason.

My lesson that I learned is that if there are 6 ICU beds, make sure you are in the top two at all times of needing care.

I have lost my patience.

# Chapter 24

# Dr. Heavy

It is no wonder that the truth

Is stranger than fiction.

Fiction has to make sense.


Mark Twain

**October 6th, 2009**

Picture this: "UGGGHHHH, ahhhhhh, OOOOOOO, UGGGGG."

Ongoing, in an infinite loop.

Well, that describes Jess's new roommate.

For twelve hours, at the top of his lungs, he is screaming in agony.

Non-stop for what seems like eternity.

Nobody acknowledges or responds to his cries.

Jess and I combined, got maybe five minutes sleep last night. Imagine that during your only five minutes sleep, you get the feeling that someone is watching you, only to open your eyes to see an old naked man, pulling an IV pole asking you for a drink of water?

This is insane.  And I also see an opening to try to get a private room.

So I buzz the nurse and explain to her that I do not feel comfortable having my daughter, who cannot move, in the same room as an old naked man that arbitrarily walks around the room at night.
For a little emphasis I add: "I don't know what I will do if it happens again."

The nurse, who says she understands, walks over to the phone in the room, picks up the receiver and says:

"Dr. Heavy to room 212 please."

Dr. Heavy is the hospital jargon for security.

"Did you just call security on me?" I bewilderingly ask.

"Mr. Passaro, we do not take lightly when someone makes a direct threat to one of our patients."

"Ok, so I get it – It is OK to have a elderly male walk around his room naked, which has a female roommate in it, but if I say "I don't know what I will do if it happens again." that I am the one who is wrong?"

After security speaks with me and realizes that I am not a terrorist or an angel killer, he shuts the lights and he leaves the room.

"UGGGHHHH, ahhhhhh, OOOOOOO, UGGGGG."
It starts again.

My first thought is that security should have taken the pillows with him.

# Chapter 25

# Red Ice at Night

Courage isn't having the strength to go on,

It is going on when you don't have the strength.

**October 9th, 2009**

Jess finally got a private room.

It took two roommates over three days, but the bottom line is that people like BettyJane more than they like me.

I am okay with that – especially when it gets the results that I want.

Yesterday, the naked old man was transferred out and a seemingly nice, but stinky old lady was transferred into Jess's room.

As is the norm, when BettyJane or I spend time at the hospital we hardly ever leave the room during our stay.

So as the seemingly nice, but stinky old lady was wheeled into the room, on the way out, the nurses taped a yellow infectious warning sign outside the entrance of the room.

I never left the room.

So I never knew that the warning sign even existed.

When BettyJane arrived, the first thing that she saw was the yellow warning sign.

The second thing that hit her was the stink.

After speaking with the nurse, BettyJane was informed that the seemingly nice, but stinky old lady has Cdiff.

CDiff is an infectious condition that spreads in a hospital setting to people on antibiotics. It causes extreme diarrhea.

Are they crazy?

It took BettyJane all of two seconds and there were plans on moving Jess to her own private room.

Just as I got to the hospital for my night shift, Jess's first night in her private room, BettyJane informs me that Jess is having a reaction to a new antibiotic that the doctors are giving her.

BettyJane let's me know that Jess has been turning red and blotchy. She said that the nurses gave her Benadryl and stopped the antibiotic, she says just keep an eye on her tonight.

I promise her that I will, as I always do.

She says – "No *really*, something is not right."

I say: "I will watch her closely."

It is now 2:00 am; I am sitting wide-awake in the dark.

Jess's heart monitor is beeping a red alert and has a 165 beats per minute reading.

That is not good.

It is not a spike reading as the reading is now increasing to 178.

I turn on the lights and I am aghast at what I see.

Jessica is BRIGHT candy apple RED, she is burning up – I'm guessing 104 to 106 degrees, easily.

Jess's eyes are just staring, hollow without any life, straight up towards the ceiling.

I run to get help, and by the time that I get back her heart rate is at 215 bpm.

Oh, I can go into every detail on how every second feels at this moment, but to summarize it -it is the worst I have felt since this ordeal began.

The top of my head, my brain, is racing trying to keep everything together.  My eyes are fighting back a dam of tears; my mouth and bottom lip can't stop quivering. My heart literally aches; my stomach feels like I have swallowed a whole bottle of vitamins on an empty stomach.

I say to myself – "No time for feeling any of this, stay poised, stay poised.  You need to take care of someone who is feeling 100x worse than you are right now."

Using Tylenol suppositories and an ice bed as their main arsenal the nurses work on Jess for what feels like hours.

Jess's heart rate slowly starts to come down, 115, 110.

Jess is in pain, she is freezing sitting naked in an ice bath.

She is screaming sounds through her trach that are absolutely heart wrenching.

She is shivering cold on the ice bed looking at me – begging me for help.

She wants off of the ice bed.

I know that leaving her in the ice will help her more than taking her out of the ice.

I do nothing, which is actually something.

I am numb.

I want to help her, so bad.

My stomach is churning, I can taste the vile as it is coming up my throat.

I keep thinking to myself a lesson that I have been taught in sports: *"That you are closer to victory than you know, when you feel that you just can't go on any longer. It is what makes champions who they are, the ability to muster up a little bit more when everyone else would give in. It is at that moment that a tipping point usually occurs."*

I say to myself – victory must be just around the corner.

# Chapter 26

# Pre

If you can fill the unforgiving minute
With sixty seconds worth of distance run,
Yours is the earth and everything that's in it,
And,

Which is more,

You'll be a man, my son!


Rudyard Kipling

**October 10th, 2009**

Nearly three decades after my wrestling career ended acrimoniously, I read something profound that Ben Askren wrote, he said:

*"That a champion is not someone who won his last match of the season, that a champion was the person who gave his all in attempting to do so."*

Yes, there can be many champions at once. Even though only one champion will be asked for his autograph, all the others will walk away with a wonderful feeling knowing that they did everything that they could have done in order to achieve their goal.

That fulfilled inner feeling is worth more than any request for an autograph.

And it lasts a lifetime.

I am walking into my boy's bedroom; it is 4:45 am. The room is a mixture of a young boys room decorated in baseball, and a teenager's room decorated in wrestling. One can tell that there was a transition in the boy's lives, somewhere around the age of twelve, as we never redecorated their room, only added to it.

I approach Travis's bed to wake him up to go to the wrestling tournament that starts in four hours, one hundred miles away.

Before I tap him on his shoulder, I notice a cloth poster hanging from his wall; one that I gave him.

It is of Steve Prefontaine, the legendary long distance runner who died too young.

It reads: "A lot of people run a race to see who is fastest, I run a race to see who has the most guts."

I reflect for a second on a lesson that I am trying to teach the boys. That sometimes you win, and sometimes you learn. That wrestling is not about beating your opponent, it is about beating yourself. To constantly push yourself to new heights, to never be content with what you have done in the past, to always strive to improve yourself, regardless of the outcome. That the outcome (win or lose) is only a focus on what you actually need to know, that a win will build confidence, but a loss builds desire. And that desire to improve is what makes champions. That in every loss there is a lesson that you need to learn, and one by one when you learn the lessons they will all come together to make you a man.

The Super 32 is less than three weeks away. The boys have been training hard. The daily devotion to the sport is about four hours a day. Our routine is that practice starts at 6:00 pm, so we arrive a half hour early, at 5:30, which means that we leave our house at 5:00. Practice ends at 8:00 pm, afterwards they hang around and we leave by 8:30. We drive to and arrive at the hospital parking lot by 9:00 pm, where I say goodbye to them, I run upstairs and within five minutes I am replaced by their mom, who takes them home.

Monday through Thursday.
Rest on Friday.
Tournament on Saturday.
Rest on Sunday.

That is the routine.

Today is Saturday.

The tournament is in Lower Hudson Valley, NY

It lasts for eight hours.

In the end, Mavericks matches pretty much all went the same way. He would start his match with his head gear on, and by the time the second period started, he would fling his head gear off during the competition as if to say "So, you want to fight eh?"

He looked good, not great. He went 4-1 with a win over a talented wrestler from Wantagh. But it is not that win that Mav will dwell on for the next week, it is the 2-1 defeat at the hands of a state qualifier from Cornwall.

Travis is on a roll. He is wrestling with an extreme amount of confidence and is in a nice rhythm. Wearing a turquoise penguin singlet and bright yellow wrestling shoes, he better back it up.

He does today.

His final's match is an overtime win over a quality wrestler from Pine Bush.

The ride home is silent.

*Winning gives you confidence, losing gives you desire.*

Travis is sleeping.

Maverick is brewing.

Maverick is sitting in the passenger seat next to me watching his match on the video camera.

At one point his opponent has a 2-1 lead, he is on the bottom, Mav on top and Mav is getting frustrated because his opponent is stalling.

Maverick is throwing cross face after cross face, inserting his elbow to his opponent's neck, he is wrenching on his opponents shoulder to score that last two points.

To quote Steve Prefontaine: "Somebody may beat me but they are going to have to bleed to do it."

Bill Bowerman, Steve Prefontaine's legendary coach at Oregon, was once asked to describe what makes Steve Prefontaine different – he replied:

"You can't teach desire."

# Chapter 27

# You Call This A Storm

I may not have gone where I intended to go,

But I think that I have ended up

Where I needed to be.


Douglas Adams

**October 11th, 2009**

When I was a kid, my mom told me the story of Roy Campanella, the Brooklyn Dodgers catcher who became paralyzed in a car crash.

I remember her telling me what was the hardest part for him to deal with during his paralysis.

It was a fly landing on his face.

He could do nothing about it.

It is Sunday morning.  I am sitting in church by myself.

A fly lands on my face.

I do nothing.  It took no more than four seconds for me to go crazy.

I consider God my friend.

I am mad at my friend right now.

And I do what one does when they are mad at their friend – I stop talking to him.

A true friend would be there in their friend's time of need; they wouldn't have to be asked, nearly begged for help, I say to myself knowing that God can hear every word.

"What is taking you so long, where are you?"

"I need help."

No answer.

I leave Mass early.

I arrive back home only to find out that my father has been admitted to the hospital.  He is in the room exactly next door to Jess.

I can't make this up.

"These footprints in the sand sure look like my shoe size…," I say to myself.

"Aren't you supposed to be carrying me?" I sarcastically add.

I drive out towards the hospital.

It is raining.

I am in my truck alone and I yell out:

"You call this a storm. It is time for a showdown, I'm right here come and get me," just like Lieutenant Dan did in Forrest Gump.

I am hurting bad, and my friend has not shown up to help me.

# Chapter 28

# An Awaiting Reservoir of "Can Do"

Nothing is impossible.

The word itself says

"I'm Possible"


Audrey Hepburn

I arrive at the hospital, as I emerge from the stairway of the second floor I am confronted by three sets of people.

My extended family informs me that my father was admitted because he is jaundice and has an abscess on his liver.

BettyJane informs me that Jess's pressure in her head has been building and is at dangerous levels and they may need to insert a shunt into her head to help drain the pressure.

And a representative from the hospital would like to speak to me, Jess's expenses are currently 2.2 million dollars above her insurance limits and they want to know how I want to handle it.

I try to look at the bright side of things and acknowledge the close proximity of my dads and Jess's rooms: "Well this is convenient, at least I don't have to travel very far to visit." I say.

I take on one problem at a time; based on the time it would take for me to solve it.

First, Mr. Representative – being that I don't have 2.2 million dollars; I don't know what I am going to do to solve that.
He hands me forms to fill out, he says that Jess is over eighteen and it is her debt, not mine, that I should fill out the forms based on Jess's assets, which there are none. Fill out these forms and return them to me in the morning, he instructs me.

I say "Ok."

As he is walking away he says: "I hear that they are looking for a rehab facility for Jess, that is good news."

I can't help myself and I mutter under my breath, "Good news for the hospital, I guess."

Problem number two. My father needs an operation on his liver to release an infection that is building up. If he does not get the operation he will die. If he does get the operation there is a 60% success rate of survival.

Seems like a no brainer to me – have the operation.

My mom doesn't want him too; she thinks that he has suffered enough.

I move onto the next problem as I know I will not be able to solve this one anytime soon.

"Did Dr. Leon talk with you?" I ask BettyJane.

"No, his associate did. Dr. Leon is on vacation."

"That is going to be a problem I say, I will only speak with Dr. Leon."

All three problems unresolved.

I now know what my next twenty-four hours will consist of.

When you dig down deep enough, you will tap into a waiting to be released reservoir of "Can Do."

It is time to do some digging.

# Chapter 29

# Dr. Dick

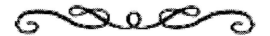

Never look back

Unless you are planning to go that way.


Henry David Thoreau

Right before BettyJane is scheduled to leave to go home, a nurse comes into our room and asks us to sign a waiver form for Jess's surgery.

"What surgery?" I ask.

BettyJane fills me in on that the doctor saw something that he didn't like and would like to do an emergency surgery on Jess to put a shunt in her head to relieve the pressure, which is building up to dangerous levels.

I ask to speak with the doctor. He is annoyed.

"Doctor, can you explain to me why Jess needs an emergency surgery?"

"Her ICP (Intracranial Pressure) was over 50 for a sustainable length of time, she is in a very dangerous zone," he says.

"When did this happen?" I ask.

"Last night – the records indicate that last night her ICP was over 50 for most of the night."

"Doctor – that information is incorrect," I inform him, sounding like Maverick in Top Gun talking to his Lieutenant Charlie about her misinformation on the MIG.

"I was with Jess all night, my eyes never left her ICP monitor, and the only time her ICP went over 50 was when she sneezed, then it went back down to 30," I let him know.

I add: "Who put that in the records – what nurse?"

He points to a nurse across the ICU, which happened to be the nurse I released and did not want on Jess's case anymore.

I say: "Doctor, I am telling you that Jess's ICP was not sustained over 50, it was 30 and spiked to 50 for thirty seconds and then came back down."

I ask to speak with Dr. Leon.

I am told that he is on vacation.

"Mr. Passaro, I do not have to explain myself to you. You do not have the intelligence that I have and unless you sign that waiver in the next five minutes your daughter will die and her blood will be on your hands, not mine," he says talking down to me.

I respond: "How dare you talk to me that way. I may not have the knowledge that you have, but I do have the intelligence. And if you want to start comparing IQ's, yours better be over 160 or I guarantee you will lose."

I go on: "Don't you ever try to make me make a decision that I am not comfortable making. I will not make a decision until I speak with Dr. Leon, and if my daughter dies in the next five minutes, well you know I can live with that, what I will not live with is dealing with a dick doctor who thinks he is holier than God."

And I walk away.

Ten minutes later Dr. Leon walks into our room.

I explain to him that the readings were not at a sustained 50 level last night. He lets me know that it is his opinion that I should go along with the surgery.

I oblige.

I ask if he is going to perform the operation and he says that he will be assisting.

I have the sudden realization that my daughters fate now lies in the hands of the doctor I just called a dick.

# Chapter 30

# Deflated

It is not what you look at that matters,

It is what you see.


Henry David Thoreau

**October 12th, 2009**

I am walking towards Jess's ICU room.

She has just come back from her operation to drain fluid from her head.

I am noticing a big difference in the way the hospital workers are looking at me as I approach Jess's room.

The look of sincere sympathy that used to be on their faces when they made eye contact with me is gone.

It has been replaced by shear helplessness as they quickly walk past me with their heads tilted down and to the right.

I feel like Bud Fox walking into his office with the Securities and Exchange Commission awaiting him.
"How could they let me walk into this room without first preparing me?" Is my first thought as I walk up to the side of the bed to give Jess a kiss hello.

My right elbow is leaning hard on Jess's mattress for support.

My head hits her hip on her bed.

I clench the bed sheets with both of my fists.

I am as close as I have ever been to giving up.

I never got pinned as a wrestler, and I refuse to be pinned now.

So I keep moving forward.

Imagine a football.

Now imagine a football that has no air in it.

That is what Jess's head looks like.

Both sides of Jess's head are touching.

From the front everything looks fine, from either side the only thing that comes to mind is the thought of "How is that possible?"

With Jess's craniotomy, which took a piece of her skull out of the side of her head, and this new operation to drain the fluid from Jess's head, Jess's head has atrophied to the point of not being recognizable as a head.

I could swear that both sides of Jess's head are meeting in the middle.

A doctor who just walked in tells me, that this is good. That this has created room in order to put Jess's bone flaps back on.

I just wish I knew what was good and what was bad.
Why is there a sudden rush to get the bone flaps back on?

What is all this sudden talk of a rehab facility?

My gut is saying that it is time to move on.

Like a gambler who is up, it is time to walk away from the table before the law of averages catches up with me.

My gut has never misled me before.

The wind has been knocked out of me.

One of my favorite quotes of all time pops into my head.

*"You can't control the wind, but you can adjust your sails."*

# Chapter 31

# We are Marshall

Clocks ticked,

But time did not pass.

The sun rose

And the sun set,

But the shadows remained.

When once there was sound

Now there was silence.

What once was whole

Now is shattered.


We Are Marshall

I am eighteen minutes into an eighteen-hour stay with Jess.

I cannot see myself lasting the remaining seventeen hours and forty-two minutes.

For the first time in the last fifty days I have crossed the line into despair.

"Hey is that you?" I hear. "I saw the name on the charts and I just had to come to your room."

The voice belongs to an old high school friend, Gina Mecca who also is a nurse in the hospital, but on a different floor.

Just like with any good friend, it didn't matter that I hadn't seen Gina in over twenty years, we start talking like we just saw each other yesterday.

We talk for a few minutes. She tells me that she is just amazed by BettyJane and myself and that the action that we have taken as parents inspires her.

Gina says good-bye and promises to stop in whenever she can.

I thank her and she departs.

She has added fuel to my empty tank.

Jess is still asleep and my mind focuses on the remainder of my shift.

Up to this point, I have never done this before, but I feel the urge to get out of the room.

I leave.

I find myself walking aimlessly throughout the hospital hallways, making wrong turn after wrong turn.

I am now somewhere where I don't know where I am, probably near the basement. I am walking down a hallway, trying not to be noticed because I know that I am probably somewhere that I shouldn't be.

There is a woman approaching me and she says "John, is that you?"

I am currently just fighting off a crying episode and didn't expect to be seen.

I lift my head and say "Yes it is."

"It's Kelly Allen from the neighborhood, what are you doing here?"

I bring Kelly up to date on what has transpired.
For the next few minutes Kelly lifts my spirits and puts more gas in my tank.

My outlook has changed.

Thanks to two people that I have not seen in over twenty years I am back on course.

Sometimes you have no idea of the impact that you can make on ones life just by being nice.

Gina and Kelly turned me around with two random acts of kindness.

Kindness that I will remember forever.

When I was on fumes, they filled my tank.

It is time to rise from the ashes.

# Chapter 32

# Love Triangle

Win you live,

Lose you die.


Tom Brands

**October 22nd, 2009**

I love my mother.

My mother loves my dad.

Those two facts are undeniable.

I want my father to live.
I want him to fight to live as long as he can.

My mother wants to let him pass.
She does not want him suffering anymore.

She says that I am not there in the middle of the night at home, when
he begs her to let him die.

I say that he should not be taking the medicine that the doctor is prescribing, that it made Mike Tyson want to eat his opponents young.

I truly do not know what my father wants, so I am going to find out.

I leave Jess's room and I enter my father's room.

It is October 22nd 2009; the Yankees are playing the Los Angeles Angels for the American League Championship Series.

I sit in a chair next to my father on the left side of his bed.

After a few minutes, my dad's gnarled four-finger hand grabs mine and does not let go.
His hand is freezing.  I can feel both bone and flesh.
There is extra space between his thumb and his middle finger, where his pointer finger used to exist.  Now there is only a nub, a casualty of the silent disease called diabetes.

As the game advances we speak about many things.
I mostly speak, he listens.
Tears slowly find their way to his ear.

I let him know that I am proud that I was able to call him my dad.

The Angels score four runs in the first inning and lead 4-0.

He gets agitated.

He says through the tubes that the Yanks will come back – that they never stop fighting.

That gives me my opening.

I ask him "Dad, do you have fight left in you?"

The tears come down at a faster pace.

His chin quivers as he nods his head up and down.

I don't know if I believe him.

Innings go by, and our conversation goes dry.

My dad's eyes are barely open as the Yankees score six runs in the top of the seventh to take the lead 6-4.
He says to me: "That's why you never quit."

It becomes too much to keep his eyes open and my dad falls asleep for the night.

Good thing, because the Angels score three runs in the bottom half of the seventh inning to win the game 7-6.

When I come back into his room to check on him the next morning he asks me a question that he already knows the answer to: "John, did the Yanks win?"

I make an exception to my no lying policy and say: "Yes, dad the Yanks won."

He asks for me to come closer, he seems annoyed.

He motions for me to come down near his head.

"John, don't you ever f*****g lie to me again." he says.

It winds up that the Angels had more fight than the Yankees did.

# Chapter 33

# Sleeping With My Sneakers On.

Nothing reduces the odds against you

Like ignoring them.

"Dr. Heavy to the Emergency Room," I hear over the loud speaker.

I comment that there must be a fight in the ER. The nurse in the room asks how I know that.

I explain to her that I have been here long enough to know all of the codes.

She doesn't believe me and sets off to stump me by asking: "Code 64?"

"Stroke," I answer.

"RRU?" she attempts again.

"Rapid Response Unit, someone is crashing."

"Dr. Pepper?"

"Fire." I reply.

"How the heck did you know that?" She was astounded.

I filled her in on my little secret. I have spent a tremendous amount of time outside in the hallway; next to the room, and that all the codes are on the phones there.

She was impressed that I memorized them all, but says to me that I could forget the Dr. Pepper code, as it has never been used before.

That is up until tonight.

It is about 4:30 am and over the loud speaker I hear: "Dr. Pepper to the ER please."

Translation – there is a fire in the Emergency Room.

That must be a false alarm I say to myself.

A nurse enters Jess's room and I ask her where the fire is?

She looked at me like I was on morphine.

"There is no fire, why would you ask that?"

I explain to her that they just called for Dr. Pepper to the ER, which means that there is a fire in the ER.

She assures me that there is no fire.

Five minutes go by, and I smell something burning, like an electric outlet smoldering.

Again I ask the nurse where is the fire, and again in return I get the look like I am delusional.

I go back to trying to go to sleep, but I am awakened by the red lights of a fire truck coming toward the hospital.

All of a sudden everyone scurries to see where the fire is.

I inform them that it is in the ER.

They look at me like - how do you know that?

I told them that it came over the loud speaker ten minutes ago.

It turns out that there was a small electrical fire in the Emergency Room that was easily put out.

I am glad.

I drill the nurses about what would happen if the fire was serious enough, what is the protocol?

A floor nurse says to me "They prioritize what patients to save first, and then they take action."

My first thought was to wonder where Jess and my dad stood on that priority list.

My second, more chilling thought was I wonder how I would have saved two virtual paralyzed family members in a fire?

I am glad I never had to find out.

I will be sleeping with my sneakers on from now on, though.

Those sneakers will now be sleeping upstate in Haverstraw, NY, where Jess is being transferred to the Helen Hayes Brain Rehabilitation facility.

Helen Hayes is one of the best Brain Injury Rehabilitation Facilities in the North East.

Ten other rehabilitation facilities turned Jess down when we applied to them. I am glad they did, or else we would never have been accepted at Helen Hayes.

Here are the terms of Jess's stay at Helen Hayes: Jess has been accepted on a thirty-day trial basis. If after thirty days Jess shows significant improvement, she stays in the program and the insurance will continue to pay for it. If she does not I will be responsible for the $2,600 per day cost of Jess's rehabilitation, which will amount to $156,000.

That is just not possible.

Also part of the terms of Jess 's stay at Helen Hayes is that normal visiting hours would not pertain to BettyJane and myself. Although we wanted twenty-four hour access to Jess, we had to settle for sixteen-hour access. BettyJane and I can be with Jess from 7:00 am until 11:00 pm, but we cannot stay the night.

I will still sleep with my sneakers on, just in case.

# Chapter 34

# Thanks Given Every Day

Not what we say about our blessings,
But how we use them,
Is the true meaning of Thanksgiving.

W.T. Purkiser

**November 26th, 2009**

I am standing in line at a Boston Market in Haverstraw, New York.

Every person in front of me is ordering turkey rather than the chicken or the meatloaf.

The workers behind the counter look like they want to be somewhere else.

The person that is ahead of me in the line is a homeless man; when he gets to the checkout counter he is given his meal for free.

He says: "Thank you," and takes his plate and sits down.

I look over my left shoulder to notice that there are at least ten people, who, like the gentleman before me, have taken their meal and have sat down by themselves to eat their Thanksgiving Day meal, alone.

I notice that some have completed their meal, but still remain in their seat because they realize that their next step is to go back outside, nowhere, into the cold.

I, myself, will take my "Family of Six" meal one mile down the road to the Helen Hayes Brain Rehabilitation Center, where I will share it with my wife and my four kids. Myself, my wife, and three of my kids will enjoy the turkey from Boston Market, while Jess will be fed her liquid Thanksgiving dinner, Jevity 2.0, through a feeding tube.

Before I walked into this Boston Market I was allowing my past experiences of Thanksgiving to dictate how I felt that this years Thanksgiving should be.

That was a mistake.

My life has changed. My life has changed a great deal.

Three months ago my daughter lost oxygen to her brain for 6 minutes.

Obviously many things in my life are not the way that I would want them to be, I am currently working on fixing that; but many things in my life have serendipitously improved a great deal, and for that I am thankful.

For one, Thanksgiving is not a once a year event.

I give thanks every day now.

Imagine if you lived your life as if it were Thanksgiving everyday, what a great life you would have.

No, this Thanksgiving will not be a traditional one, one where most family members are forced to spend a few hours with each other over dinner, and are too glad to get out of that setting because they just can't take each others company anymore without fighting, over nothing.

No, this Thanksgiving I get to spend time with my family, eating Boston Market in the lounge of a hospital and savoring every moment of it.

Watching the traditional Detroit Lions football game this year has been replaced with a pick up basketball game that my family plays on a court outside of the facility. My youngest daughter, Cassidy, who is six, makes the game winning shot – a pure swish on a ten-foot basket.

Her first swish ever.

I am overwhelmed with joy for being able to experience her first swish ever.

Like I said, my life has changed.

My life has changed a great deal.

For the better.

# Chapter 35

# REM – Losing My Religion

Oh life, It's bigger
It's bigger than you
And you are not me
The lengths that I will go to
The distance in your eyes.

That's me in the corner.

That's me in the spotlight.

I thought that I heard you laughing
I thought that I heard you sing
I think I thought I saw you try
But that was just a dream
Try, cry, why try
That was just a dream
Just a dream
Just a dream, dream.

REM

Losing My Religion

**November 27th, 2009**

It has been a little over one month since the Angels came back to beat the Yankees in the 5th game of the American League Championship Series.

BettyJane and I are both in the same location outside of Jess's hospital room together for only the third time.

We are standing in line and are both holding a single red rose in each of our right hands.

Again.

I am standing at the end of the line, which is slowly moving forward.

I have not had REM sleep for months.

I look to BettyJane and say to her: "Do you know what I really miss?"

"Besides, Jess, Terri and your dad?" she reminds me.

"I miss dreaming. I haven't dreamt in three months.
Every night I am totally blank, nothing, nada.
I miss dreaming."

She agrees and adds: "We have had no time to dream in this nightmare."

We walk arm in arm back to the limo.

I feel nothing and I hate it.

If given a choice between grief and nothing, I would choose grief.

I have no hurt left. It has been all used up.

Where is my friend?

# Chapter 36

# The Look

Unless someone like you cares a whole awful lot,

Nothing is going to get better.

It's not.


Dr. Seuss

The Lorax

**November 28th, 2009**

It is less than twelve hours since I vaguely remember saying goodbye to my father.

I am now arriving back in Haverstraw where I am on my way to spend the day with Jess.

My mind makes a mental note that I forgot to thank Patti, a good friend, who stayed with Jess, so BettyJane and I could say goodbye to my father together.

Before I head out to Helen Hayes I want to go down the road and get a cup of coffee at Dunkin Donuts.

I am running late.

I know the round trip will probably take 15 minutes, factoring in the traffic, the line at Dunkin Donuts and me needing to be able to finish drinking the coffee before I enter Jess's room, which will all definitely make me later.

I decide to go anyway.

I get in my car and head to Dunkin Donuts. The one-mile trip takes less than three minutes. There is no traffic.

I get out of my car and I enter the store. It is empty. It is 6:55 am and there is not a soul in Dunkin Donuts getting coffee.

Life is different in Haverstraw.

Back downstate, if I entered a Dunkin Donuts at 6:55 am, and it was empty, I would immediately vacate the premises fearing that there were hostages being held in the back room somewhere.

There is one person working in the store, a vibrant thirty something year old young lady who immediately greets me with "Hi, my name is Wanda, isn't today a great day?"

I nod, as small talk by my nature does not come naturally to me.

"You're not from around here, are you?" she says with confidence.

"No, I am not," I respond, still not opening up.

There is some silence – I fear that I have hurt her feelings with my short answers so I ask her out of guilt: "How did you know that?"

She smiles, which makes me seem like I caught on to the fact that whether I liked it or not, that we were going to have a conversation before I got any service.

"You're a HHH person," she says as if she is putting the pieces together as she is saying this.

"I'm a what?"

"A HHH person – A Helen Hayes on the Hill person." She queues me in on the meaning of her acronym.

"You have a loved one at Helen Hayes, right?" she asks me for confirmation.

"Who is it?" she asks as if it really means something to her.

"It is my daughter." I say choked up.

"What is her name?" Wanda asks.

"Her name is Jessica." I proudly say.

"What a beautiful name – you do know what Jessica means, don't you?"

My first thought is "Who is this girl?" which I silently ask only to myself.

My second thought, which I vocalize, is "No, I really don't know what it means."

It means: "She knows," she says.

"She knows," she says again.
"How did you know I was a HHH person?" I ask, now opening up.

"You have *the look*," Wanda enlightens me. "You see I had the same look a few years back when my brother was at Helen Hayes after a motorcycle accident."

There is a brief silence and then Wanda says to me "It hurts, doesn't it?"

My chin quivers and I hurry to say "Yes it does," before I have to step away to hide my tears.

I fear to know how her brother is doing now; being that she didn't offer, I do not ask.

"Remember – she knows," she says again.

"Thank you," I say.

I take my coffee, and drive back to HHH. The round trip wound up taking 15 minutes, but for much better reasons than traffic and crowds.

I walk into the lobby at Helen Hayes, and even though I am running late I make a detour to the gift shop in the lobby as some pajamas with a motivational saying on them catches my eye in the window.

I head to the back of the store to find the unique pajamas, instead I find a pregnant woman visibly upset, with *the look*.

"Hi my name is John," I say totally against my nature.

"Are you OK?"

"Hi John, my name is Bridgett and I am not OK, but thank you for asking."

Some silence fills the air.

"What loved one do you have here?" I ask.

"My husband – how about you?"

"My daughter," I respond back.

"It hurts, doesn't it?" I vulnerably share.

"Yes it does," Bridgett says. "But it hurts less now." Bridgett smiles.

We both separate from the back of the store and head our separate ways.

I wind up not getting the motivational pajamas that I saw in the window and I head up to Jess's community room.

I am sitting bedside with Jess, holding her hand, when Bridgett walks into the room.

She sits down next to her husband, and she moves his hand and places it on her lap.

After a few moments, Bridgett picks up her head, she sees me across the room and recognizes me from the gift shop.

She then smiles and silently mouths "Thank You."

Bridgett has a new look.

# Chapter 37

# Only Light Drives Out Darkness

Walking with a friend in the dark,

Is better than walking alone in the light.


Helen Keller

**November 29th, 2009**

The emotional dichotomy of my days is torturous.

So much has happened.
So little has happened.

Time has stood still.
Time has flown by.

BettyJane and I are hopeful.
And many days we are crushed and broken down to our core.

It is 6:00 am and I am getting my day started.

I am in a 10x10 former dorm room, which has two small beds, a small refrigerator, a television, two pink concrete walls and two walls that have windows to the outside, which are covered by old venetian blinds.

This dorm room is exactly one hundred feet directly across the parking lot of Helen Hayes Rehabilitation facility and exactly one hundred miles from my home.

Helen Hayes is nice enough to allow BettyJane and myself to use this dorm room on campus, like a Ronald McDonald House while we visit Jess. It saves us paying for a hotel for the next ninety days. I am very appreciative, and I silently pledge to myself that when I become rich I will start a similar program one day.

Being that Jess is over a hundred miles from our home BettyJane and I decide to take four-day shifts at a time.

I am about to leave the dorm room to start mine.

The cornerstone of my faith is my belief that: "Everything in life happens for a reason" and that "God works in mysterious ways."

My faith and belief system are being tested and I need a sign.

So I ask for one.

I just blurt it out, sort of what someone does when they start talking to someone that they haven't spoken to in a while.

"I need a sign. I need something. I'm not asking for much, but you got to give me something."

I try to use leverage that I do not have as I plead: "Please show me a clear, distinct, undeniable sign by midnight tonight."

I wipe my eyes, pick up my key off of the refrigerator top and I head over to see Jess.

I open the door to the facility and I walk through the beautiful marble lobby to the elevator.

I am alone in the elevator on the way up to Jess's room.

Hanging on the walls of the elevator is the state mandated results and data from all the Brain Rehabilitation Centers in New York State. I find it odd that Helen Hayes is ranked below average in almost every category.

"That can't be," I think to myself. "It must be that they get the more severe cases," I rationalize to myself.

The elevator dings when it gets to the 3rd floor, I get out and walk towards Jess's room.

I have been told to measure Jess's progress over months and years and not over days.

That is all good, except for the fact that Jess has days here and not months or years.

Jess needs to start fast and show improvement quickly.

Against my best wishes Jess is sharing a room with three other patients who have also have a trach.

I enter the room.

There is a huge window that takes up the whole far wall. It allows a tremendous amount of sunshine into the room but makes the room extremely hot.

Jess's bed is on the far right hand side of the room.

Directly across from her is Zorie. Zorie is a middle age African American woman who recently had a stroke. Zorie's neck is tilted from the stroke and is almost perpendicular with her body. It is hard to view.

Next to Jess is Crystal. Crystal is a twenty-year-old young girl who can pass for eight. Crystal lives near by and her mom and family visit her often.

Directly across from Jess, is Chris. A few months ago, while Chris was on the construction site helping to build the New Yankee Stadium, Chris's head got crushed between two steel beams. Chris has an extensive brain injury and a pregnant wife named Bridgette.

The first day that I entered this room I only saw the disability of each person.

Today I see four people who happen to have a disability.

As I walk in, I do what I normally do to start the day; I turn on everyone's television to the right channel for that person even though each person is either in a coma or has an extensive brain injury.

Crystal gets Nickelodeon, Chris gets the football channel, Zorie gets the soaps and Jess gets the fashion channel.

I keep my eyes open for the sign.

Overall I know that Jess is getting better.

Jess's schedule for the day is intense. She has two physical therapy sessions, two speech therapy sessions, and two occupational therapy sessions.

Jess has taken to some therapists and hates others.

It is a long day that ends around 3:00 pm.

By this time Jess is mentally and physically exhausted and is prepared for bed.

Normal visitation hours are over now, and I am the only parent left in the room.

My mind has stopped looking for any sort of sign.

Jess has been given her "medicine" and she is fast asleep and will be for the rest of the night.

I sit by her bedside until I am asked to leave about 11:00 pm.

I kiss Jess on the forehead and I head back to the room.

On the way out, when I am in the elevator, I realize that I have not eaten at all today. There are not many food places that are open at this hour in Haverstraw, but I find one.

I order my meal and I sit in my car and I eat it.

I take my time, as I have nowhere else to go.

The clock on the dashboard says 12:01 am.

I head back to the room.

It is cold and pitch black outside. There is no sign of life anywhere.

There are three sets of doors to my room.

I juggle for my keys, which are hard to handle with my gloves on.

I enter the first set of doors, which takes me into the dorms hallway.

A few feet down on the left hand side, I unlock another door, which takes me into a vestibule and a quad of rooms.

The last key is inserted and I open the door to my room.
It is pitch black inside.

Except for an illuminating ray of light that is coming from the lamppost outside, shining through my window, filtered by a cracked venetian blind, which has beamed a perfect white cross on the pillow of my bed.

I stare in disbelief.

"Thank you, my friend," I say out loud.

There are a few things that I now know.

I know that I have a friend and that somehow, someway; something good is going to come out of this. I don't know why so much pain and suffering needs to be involved, but I am certain that "Everything happens for a reason" and "God works in mysterious ways."

For the first time in a long time, I do not want the sun to rise any time soon, for I have found my light in the darkness, and it feels real good.

# Chapter 38

# From Melrose Place to ER overnight

I long to accomplish

A great and noble task,

But it is my chief duty

To accomplish small tasks,

As if they were great and noble.


Helen Keller

**November 30th, 2009**

Jess and I are sitting in the dining room of Helen Hayes.

Jess is in a form fitted wheelchair and I am sitting next to her in an equally uncomfortable chair.

We are looking out through a beautiful window, which overlooks the mountains outside. It is a beautiful site, which must be unimaginably gorgeous in early autumn.

In about five minutes I am going to take Jess inside where the therapists will attempt to red plug Jess's trach.

Basically, they will take out the tube that is coming out of Jess's throat right above her chest and they will insert a red plug thus allowing Jess to breath on her own without any help for the first time in 110 days.

This is a huge step.

Jess and I glance outside one last time.

I wheel Jess back into her room as her therapist is waiting.

The therapist quickly takes the tube out from Jess's throat and inserts the red plug.

You should see the look on Jess's face.

Her facial expression is screaming out:

"I love this. This breathing stuff is great. I can't believe I took this for granted before. I will never do that again."

Jess sits there appreciating every drop of oxygen that goes into her nose and into her lungs.

She is glowing; a breath of life has come over her face.

After five minutes the therapist unplugs the red plug and reinserts the tubing into Jess's throat, and says "We don't want to over do it today."

Jess starts to cry.
Real tears.

I try to keep Jess's positive momentum rolling.

I say "Jess, I am going to ask you some questions and I want you to answer them by blinking once for "yes" and twice for "no"."

I give her some time to adjust and get ready.

"First question Jess – You and I used to watch a TV show together when you were younger.  Was the name of that show 90210?"

I pause and Jess blinks twice.

"Or was the name of the show Melrose Place?"

One blink.

I am astounded.  That is correct.

"During that show you and I ate some food.  Was that food Popcorn?"

Two blinks.

"Or was it Chocolate Chip cookies?"

One blink – Correct.

I ask Jess a series of eighteen questions; she answers sixteen of them correctly with her eyes.

I do not want this day to end.

Across the room I hear a cough.

That is not good.

It is almost 3:00 pm and time to get ready for bed.

I stay until 11:00 pm as I usually do, with Jess never opening up her eyes after 3:30 pm.

It is now 5:00 am of the next morning and my cell phone is ringing. "Mr. Passaro, Jessica ran a high fever last night, she vomited, aspirated and we had to take her to the ER, where she is now."

It is snowing outside; there is almost six inches already on the ground. I make the twenty-minute trip to the local hospital in two hours.

On the way I call BettyJane and inform her of last nights events.

She is on her way.

I just can't believe in less than twenty-four hours Jess went from Melrose Place to the ER.

# Chapter 39

# Certifiably Insane

The distance between insanity and genius

Is measured only by success.

**December 5th, 2009**

As I am driving home from Helen Hayes, somewhere near the George Washington Bridge my mind shifts from Jess and starts to focus on Maverick, Travis and Cassidy.

The Super 32 has come and gone and the boys did not participate in this year's tournament.

When it was time to leave to attend the tournament a few weeks ago, both Maverick and Travis came up to me and said that they did not want to go.

They felt that it was more important that I stay with my dad in the hospital, as they knew his time was fast approaching.

*"We can go next year, and the year after that, Dad."*
*"You will not be able to see grandpa ever again."*
*"We need to stay home dad."*

And we did.

The high school wrestling season started three weeks ago.

I arrive back on Long Island just in time to pick up Maverick and Travis from wrestling practice.

Maverick approaches the car, the skin on his face is hugging his cheekbones very tightly, his pants are falling off of him, and he can barely talk because his mouth is so dry.

It dawns on me that certifications are tomorrow.

How no one has called Child Protective Services on me is amazing, I think to myself.

Maverick has literally not eaten in two weeks. His weight has dropped from 132 pounds to 112 pounds over that short time.

Just in the last four days since I have been gone he has gotten noticeably skinnier.

Tomorrow the boys will provide a urine sample, get weighed and have a skin fold test to measure their percentage of body fat.

The urine sample determines whether or not a wrestler is hydrated, the skin fold test provides the numbers that determine whether a wrestler can "safely" lose any more weight.

I am looking at Maverick right now and he is not in any safe zone.

There is no way that he is hydrated and his percentage of body fat is at dangerously low levels.

I can tell that with my own eyes, I do not need an official reading from any caliper to convince me of that.

Travis is able to wrestle in the 96-pound weight class without having to lose any weight.

He looks normal.

The boys come home and do what every wrestler does before an event.

They go up to their rooms, crash in their beds and they curl up in a ball until the morning.

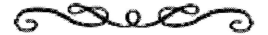

It is now the morning and we are on our way to East Islip High School for the 2009-2010 Official High School Certifications.

My eyes prove me right.

Maverick has failed his hydration test miserably and his body fat is at 5%, which is insane.

There is an appeal process for the hydration test in three days.

It would mean that Maverick would have to hold his weight by not eating or drinking for another three days, and somehow be hydrated.

Insanity is doing the same thing over and over again and expecting different results.

If left up to his decision, Maverick would continue pursuing getting certified to wrestle at 112 pounds.

I step in and without asking him; let him know that the pursuit is over.

It is time to go up a weight class.

After two minutes of convincing him, Maverick is now a 119 pounder.

I believe that I made the right decision, even though he will have two State Champions in his weight class at 119 pounds; it is his overall health that I am more worried about.

I look around at all the wrestlers who are excruciatingly thin and wonder to myself how this certification process actually stops them from cutting an insane amount of their body weight.

It does not.

At least both Maverick and Travis will be able to eat for the next three months.

The 2009-2010 Section XI High School Season has officially begun.

# Chapter 40

# A Pair of 2's

It is not about the cards you are dealt,

It is about how you play the hand.

Randy Pausch

The Last Lecture

**December 21st, 2009**

I am standing in a corner, in a hallway, outside of Jess's room at Helen Hayes.

It is where I go to gather myself when I am overwhelmed.
Jess is back here at Helen Hayes after overcoming another bout of pneumonia.

This corner is more of an alcove, than a corner, as it has a ledge on the radiator on which I can sit, and a floor to ceiling window, in which I can view the beautiful upstate mountains and late autumn landscape.

Jess is currently inside, lying down on a board. Two therapists, one on each side of her, are standing the board upright to "stand" Jess up.

She is held in place by three Velcro straps, one each around her chest, hips and ankles.

The two therapists simultaneously lift the board up and stop when they get to 45 degrees; they pause for a moment and then take Jess the full 90 degrees upright.

Initially, I am elated that Jess is out of bed for the first time in 100 days.

Then it hits me, in order to get out of bed she needed to be velcroed to a board and stood up by two therapists.

Hence, I am outside in the hallway gathering myself and trying to adjust my train of thought.

As I look out through the window into the horizon, a huge spider is weaving a gigantic web on the outside of the window, three stories above the ground, clouds my view.

I chuckle to myself as a childhood memory of "Charlottes Web" enters my mind.

At first, the reference sweeps through my mind and tries to leave, but at the last second I pull it back into my head.

I believe that there are no coincidences in life, only subtle signs that when you inspect them will lead you to where you need to go.

This spider is three stories above the ground spinning his web in front of me for a distinct reason.

I believe that.

I stare into the vast web for what seems like a few minutes, looking for a word and or the spiders' message.

I don't see any words or messages.

So I close my eyes, I still my mind, and I wait until the message comes to me.
I still don't see anything.

Could it be that there is no message, that there is nothing to learn from my current situation?  That it is all just a meaningless tragedy?

I don't believe that.

I bring my body to a deep rest and I listen.

"22" appears.

I don't know what that means.

"22 what?"

Then it dawns on me.

It is not "22", but rather a pair of 2's.

One of the worst hands that you can be dealt in poker.

A pair of 2's.  Just enough to go on, but almost a sure loser.

My spirits are dampened.

"You're kidding me? That is the motivational saying that my personal Charlotte weaves me in my mind – that I have been dealt a bad hand?"

"I already know that – that is not new news.  That is not inspiring, that is just plain mean and piling on to someone when he is down."

All day it bothers me;  "22" has to mean something else.
It can't mean that I have been dealt a bad hand – that is too obvious.

After subconsciously searching my mind all day, it finally comes to me:

The best poker players find a way to win with any hand that they are dealt.

My subconscious mind also provides me with an overwhelmingly personal example to prove its point.

A few years ago back in my baseball coaching days; I spent two weeks in Florida with my boys for an AAU National Championship Tournament. During those two weeks, to pass time, the team played its share of Texas Hold'em Poker at night.

I remember winning my most rewarding hand with a pair of 2's!

I remember bluffing my last opponent, who held 3 Aces, out of the hand to win the biggest pot of the trip.

As he went out, he asked to see my hand. As I showed him my pair of 2's he scowled:

"A Pair of 2's?!"

"You won the biggest hand of the last two weeks with a pair of 2's?!"

I remember saying, "It's not the cards that you are dealt, it's how you play your hand," as I reached into the middle of the table and pulled my reward in closer to me.

*"It's not the cards that you are dealt, it's how you play your hand,"*

I need to bluff life right now.

I need to act as if I am holding 4 Aces.

I need to make every one of my moves with extreme confidence.

*I need to act as if…*

I need to detach all negativity, unplug the pain, cut off all ties to sadness, run away from bitterness and tackle my grief.

I need to do and feel the opposite of what a normal person would feel in these circumstances, because if I just stand pat and play this hand that life has dealt me like life expects me too; I will go out with a pair of 2's.

I need to win this hand.

So I am going ALL IN.

Yes, I am going to exude confidence, push everything to the limit, and I am not going to blink under the pressure. I am going to play this hand as if it is a sure winner.

I am going to win the hand that life has dealt me, with a pair of 2's!

And it is going to be very rewarding.

# Chapter 41

# Every Thorn Has a Rose.

Those things, which are precious

Are saved only by sacrifice.


David Kenyon Webster

**December 24th, 2009**

It is Christmas Eve.

It is lightly snowing.

There is a heavy layer of snow on the ground, on top of snow that has been there for a few weeks already.

I pull my car into the parking lot and I get out.

I am walking towards a beautifully decorated building.

Every tree that leads up to it is shining in the dark and glimmering in beautiful white lights.

It is gorgeous.

It is Good Samaritan Hospital in Nyack, New York.

Jess is back in the hospital.

In Jess's thirty-six day stay at Helen Hayes so far, twenty-four have been in this hospital.

Helen Hayes has some great points and one major flaw.

They refuse to listen that Jess cannot be in a community room.

This is Jess's third bout with pneumonia caused by an infection from the tubing of her trach.

They refuse to take the trach out; they say she is not ready to breathe on her own.

I beg to differ.

I say that the trach, if left in, is going to be the cause of her death.

I am carrying a very large Alaskan Malamute stuffed animal, as I enter Jess's room the first thing that I see is that Jess's medical chart is inside of a stocking and is hanging on the wall.

BettyJane is sitting on the windowsill and she is looking outside at the beautiful scenery.

She is biting what is left of her nails.

She does not realize that I am here.

How I wish I could make her stop hurting.

Even just for a day.

She finally turns around and says:

"Let's put Jess in the car and go home. We can't do this anymore."

"First it was Thanksgiving at Boston Market, now its Christmas in the hospital – this is not what a family is about."

I say: "Just the opposite – It is exactly what family is about."

I convince BettyJane that we will take Jess home, just not today.

But very, very soon, I promise her.

She hugs me, picks up her suitcase and heads out to her car.

I watch from the windowsill as she passes each of the beautifully lit trees, opens her car door, hesitates and then slowly drives away.

Somehow after she leaves the scenery does not seem as beautiful.

# Chapter 42

# Mrs. Irrelevant

When it comes to life

The critical thing is

Whether you take things for granted

Or have gratitude for the opportunity.

Gilbert K. Chesterton

Every year over three hundred players are selected in the NFL college draft.

One of them has to hold the dubious distinction of being the last player selected.

Each year that player is nicknamed "Mr. Irrelevant" because no one really expects the last player selected to ever make an impact with any team in the NFL.

In 1983, that honor belonged to John Tuggle, whom the NY Giants drafted with the 335th overall and last pick of that year's draft.

Irrelevant is defined as insignificant, unimportant, immaterial and easily overlooked.

John Tuggle was anything but irrelevant, insignificant, unimportant, immaterial or easily overlooked.

The 1983 "Mr. Irrelevant" became the first player in NFL history to make the roster of the team that selected him in the draft. John not only made the team, but he also made an impact - earning the New York Giants Special Teams Player of the Year, in his rookie season.

John's biggest impact would come off of the field though, in the real game of life.

The following year during a routine physical for the team, John Tuggle was diagnosed with a rare form of cancer.

He would never play again.

For the next two years no teammate dared to complain about a sprained ankle or a sore rib as they witnessed John battle and practice with the team everyday in an attempt to recapture his starting position, while losing his hair, being sapped of his energy and battling cancer, all at the same time.

John's will and determination touched every one of his teammates, and especially his soon to be Hall of Fame coach.

Even though John would never play another down in the NFL and would die in his sleep a few years later, "Mr. Irrelevant" made a significant impact, in the most important area:

On other peoples lives.

The 335th pick of the 1983 NFL college draft, wound up being anything but irrelevant.

His Hall of Fame coach, Bill Parcells, said this of John:

*You had to gain an understanding of this guy's determination, his will. You gain an appreciation for those qualities only under duress, during times of pain. John had qualities that you couldn't see. John Tuggle has made a great impact on my life.*

**December 25th, 2009**

Once again the dreadful combination of lack of mobility, and an open hole in her throat, has landed Jess in the hospital with another bout of pneumonia.

I am getting to be a pro at this by now – by this, I mean my three day excursion staying in Jess's hospital room with her, being her advocate while she is as vulnerable as one could possibly be.

At first I would just blend in and just be there for Jess and allow the hospital to run on its rhythm.

It didn't take me too long to figure out that the cookie cutter system that the hospital ran on was not what was right for Jess. While having a respiratory treatment done at midnight, blood work done at 2 am, temperature taken at 4 am and blood pressure taken at 6 am may have been what was right for the hospital, it certainly was not the schedule that I felt was right for Jess.

She needed uninterrupted rest to heal.

So I quarantined her.

I made it perfectly clear that no one was allowed in her room from 11 pm until 8 am, so she could get her proper rest.

Utopia ensued after this adjustment; or as close to Utopia as I could create under the circumstances.

After a few attempts of trying to ignore my new quarantine rules, the hospital adjusted to my new schedule for Jess.

So at exactly 8 am, on Christmas morning, a very reluctant head peaked into Jess's room and said: "Mr. John, would you mind if I came in and cleaned the room?"

It was Juanita.

"No, of course not Juanita, come on in."

During my multiple stays at the hospital to date, Juanita and I have exchanged pleasantries as she cleaned Jess's room – she always brought happiness with her on any day that I saw her.

"It is such a beautiful day today, sun shining early in the morning; it reminds me of back home." She shares.

To myself I ask how Juanita can be in such a great mood as she is working on Christmas morning.

Outwardly I inquire, "Where is back home?"

"San Pedro de Macoris."

"No way - your from San Pedro de Macoris?" I blurt out as if I was born there.

"You know?" She asks surprisingly.

"Of course I know – it is the 'cradle of shortstops' – more major league shortstops come from San Pedro de Macoris than from any other town on earth," I share with her my trivia knowledge of her infamous hometown.

"Yes, yes, you know."

"Juanita – how do they do it, how does your hometown produce such great ballplayers?"

"Mr. John, I no live there for a long time but I do still have family there," she responds.

I ask a different way "Juanita when you lived there – what was it like?"

"Ohh, very poor – everyone is very poor. I remember little boys not having enough money for a ball, so they used a sock. They played all day. They loved to play. They all want to be – how you say – All Star?"

"Yes an All Star," I confirm.

She goes on "The boys play in their bare feet in the streets all day, they love to play. There is nothing else. They can't believe that America pays boys millions of dinero to play baseball – a game that they would play for nada."

For a brief second, I contemplate how miraculous it is for a boy from San Pedro de Macoris to make it to the major leagues.

"Juanita, you said that you have family back home?" I ask.

"Yes Mr. John – my son, he not a baseball boy. I am so glad that I have this job at Hospital – I save money to send to him for him to come to America one day."

"It must be hard to be away from your family," I solemnly say.

"Mr. John, I know my boy is ok – one day I will see him again. That will be a great day."

She adds, "Mr. John, I watch you – you a good man. Always here with sweet Jess, never leave room."

Then she stuns me by saying: "Me and you are the same – we see opportunity. We both be with our kids again one day. Until that day I keep working and send money back home, and you keep being a good man. It will happen – I promise."

Somehow, I truly believe her.

Juanita has a quality that you can't see. She has made my life better.

From San Pedro De Macoris to the Majors, for both of us.

# Chapter 43

# Adult Large – Take the Hit

Hold on

Hold on to yourself

For this is gonna hurt like hell.


Sarah McLaughlin

Hold On

**December 28th, 2009**

Every once in a while I just need to be anonymous, invisible to everyone so I can rejuvenate my batteries to be able to fight my daily battle.

The super hero power that I wish for the most is not from Superman or Spiderman; it is from Bert from Soap - the ability to cross my forearms in front of my chest and snap my fingers and become invisible.

Just for a few minutes.

To be able to create a protective shield around me where nothing can get in, just for enough time for me to regain my composure and continue fighting.

Sometimes I do this by sitting in my car by myself before I head back into my house after going to the market, or sometimes I stroll outside and wander for a few minutes.

A few minutes of solitude does wonders for me.

Today, something told me, as I was driving home from the hospital, that I should become invisible at Boston Market before going home.

It didn't make any sense, as dinner was waiting for me.

So I enter the restaurant, I find an out of the way table in the corner, and I become invisible.

Or so I thought.

As I was sitting down biting into my Chicken Carver sandwich I see "Adult Large's" dad walk through the vestibule, look around the store and immediately make a beeline towards me.

I guess my super powers of invisibility are not working today.

I fondly call him, "Adult Large's" dad because six years ago when I was helping to run the Little League in my town and we were placing orders for our Major League Replica uniforms at 2 am in the morning, we came across an order for a "L" jersey for a player. The order did not specify if it should be a youth large or an adult large sized jersey. Being that there was no phone number on the application, and the order had to be in the first thing in the morning, we needed to make an executive decision.

We ordered an adult large custom Major League replica jersey.

For the smallest kid in the league.

The jersey acted like a parachute as he ran the bases.

Hence the name "Adult Large."

It has been six years since I have seen "Adult Large's" dad.

He is now standing over my shoulder and asks, "Do you mind if I sit down?"

"Please do," I respond.

I find it weird that he does not order any food.

He starts out by saying "You know I have never been in a Boston Market in my entire life." He pauses and adds, "I was driving around aimlessly and something told me to stop, I didn't know why until I got to the door and I saw you."

He now has my attention.

"I am really sorry to hear about Jess," he says with genuine sadness.

"Thank you," I say.

"How is little Johnny?" I inquire.

"He is killing me and my family, he has lost his way," he bluntly shares with me.

"That is the reason that I was driving around tonight – I just had to leave the house, its bad. Real bad."

He adds, "I have done everything that I could possibly do – I'm done. Do you know that he just came at me with a bat?"

I can see that he is at the end of his line and that this is dominating his life.

He confesses: "I am walking away from him – what else am I supposed to do?"

"Take the hit." I say.

"What do you mean, 'take the hit?'"

"I mean, when he comes after you with the bat 'take the hit,'" I say with passion.

"Are you crazy? That would hurt so much – he would break my ribs," he spurts out.

"You are right, it is going to hurt like hell. But your ribs will eventually heal.

If you walk away I guarantee you that it will hurt much more than broken ribs and that that hurt will never go away."

I pause and I say it again, "Take the hit."

"Take the hit," he slowly says to himself.

"Whose team are you on?" I ask him.

"I don't follow you – what do you mean whose team am I on?" he asks.

"I mean, you want your son back and there are forces in this world that want to take him from you. There is a battle going on. Sides have been taken, John's team is his family and the other team is everything that you don't want for your son. Walking away is the exact thing that the other side wants. Instead of walking away, you need to fight."

I add: "Treat a man as he is, and he will remain as he is. Treat a man as he could be and he will become what he should be." I have no idea where that just came from but it just effortlessly flowed out of my mouth. It must have been the hundreds of hours of reading at Jess's bedside that I have been doing.
"I am telling you and I need for you to listen – Don't you ever walk away from your son, no matter what he has done. You need to fight to get him back. You are on his team, not there's."

Before my eyes, I could see what once was a smoldering fire, that was ready to be put out, turn back into a flame.  Adult Large's dad's eyes and heart are alive again, saved from the circumstances of life.

"Adult Large's" dad and I wind up speaking until there are no other patrons in the restaurant.

As we eventually get up to leave, we both acknowledge to each other that we were both meant to find each other on this night.

I cross my arms across my chest, snap my fingers - it is time to go home and eat dinner.

# Chapter 44

# Nurse Ratched

But it is the truth,

Even if it didn't happen.


One Flew Over the Cuckoos Nest.

**January 4ᵗʰ, 2010**

Crystal is shaking.

There is a flurry of nurses running to her bed.

It is 10:45 pm and I am the only non Helen Hayes employee in the room.

It is one day since Jess is back from the hospital; now back in her community room at Helen Hayes.

I try not to watch directly as the nurses and doctors work feverishly to try to bring Crystal out of her seizure.

It is heart breaking to watch.

Finally, after fifteen minutes, Crystal stops.

She is calm and immediately goes into a deep sleep.

I leave.

It is now 10:00 am and Crystal's mother is entering the room to visit.

"So how was Crystal's night?" she asks a nurse.

"She slept like a baby," the nurse replies as she slightly tilts her head and sees me sitting next to Jess in the background and remembers my presence there last night.

"That's good," Crystal's mom says.

I slightly shake my head to myself.

By noon I am informed that I need to adhere to the official parents visiting hours going forward and that it is only right that I allow other parents to use the dorm room too.

It is now time to go home.

I inform Nurse Ratched, who just installed these new terms and conditions, to start the paperwork for Jess's release.

"What nursing home would you like us to make the transfer too."

"The loving home of John and BettyJane Passaro," I reply.

# Chapter 45

# A New Set Of Problems

Do what you can,

With what you have,

Where you are.


Theodore Roosevelt

**January 9th, 2010**

For the second time in the last 140 days there is an ambulance parked outside my house.

This time, Jess is being taken out of the back of the ambulance and into our home.

For the first time in the last 140 days BettyJane and I are fighting.

She cannot believe that while she was driving down in the ambulance with Jess, that I, along with our two friends Patti and Carl, rearranged (emptied) her dining room and turned it into a hospital room for Jess.

She wanted everything put back in its original place.

The fight was not about what Patti, Carl and myself did to the dining room; the fight was about BettyJane's sudden realization that our house will never be normal again.  Our house is now part hospital, part house, and that realization hit BettyJane hard.

The good news is that Jess is home, finally after 140 days.

The bad news is that our house is not handicap accessible, there is no place to bathe Jess, and no place that she can have her own privacy.

There is also no place for Maverick, Travis and Cassidy to live normally, no place that they can entertain friends, that they can watch TV or not be affected by the new environment inside of their house.

I just know one thing; I love having these new problems, because finally, Jess is back home.

# Chapter 46

# Magic Wand

I wish I had a magic wand
That I could use each day.
A wand that held the kind of magic
To make sadness go away.

The Magic Wand

Jack R. Roberts

**February 16th, 2010**

My mind is in overdrive, and I cannot sleep.

I grab my laptop and attempt to go online to pass the time.

As I open the top of the laptop up, the screen automatically goes on.

There is a half written letter on the screen.

*Dear Extreme Makeover,*

*My name is Maverick Passaro and I live in Long Island, NY.*

*I have decided to write to you to tell you about the two heroes' in my life –
my mom and dad.*

*My parents would sacrifice anything for my brothers and sisters and me.*

*Now it is my turn to try and help them.*

*My parents have never been big on fixing up our house; they have always
spent the money instead on us. I can't tell you the amount of things that
need to be fixed in our house.*

*You would never know it from looking at our house from the outside.*

*On the inside it needs repair.*

*But for us, that has always been ok.*

*That is not why I am writing to you today.*

*On August 22nd our lives changed when my nineteen-year-old sister went
into cardiac arrest – she is now nearly paralyzed.*

*For four months my mom and my dad never left her side. I mean never, 24
hours per day, every day.*

*They both took shifts in a hospital upstate while the other tried to keep
everything together back home. One of my parents was always with Jess,
and the other was always with us.*

*Everyone told them to put Jess in a nursing home, but they said that Jess is
part of our family and that she belongs home with us.*

*Now on top of everything, my sister's room was upstairs, she is now living
in our dining room with no privacy at all, I don't know how she will ever
shower because the only shower is upstairs and we can't get Jess up and
down the stairs at all.*

*My dad sleeps on the floor next to her at night and my mom sleeps upstairs.*

*My mom and dad are struggling with everything that is going on, so I am sure that we will not be able to build a shower downstairs anytime soon. My parents are so overwhelmed but yet they take each day and make it the best that they can, not knowing what to expect from tomorrow, with hope that the next upcoming day will be better.*

*If you could please help make their lives a little easier, I would feel like somehow I have helped them.*

*When someone asks my mom "Is there anything I can do for you?" she always answers with a tear in her eye: "Do you have a magic wand?"*

*Maybe you can be that magic wand.*

*Or that angel from "It's a Wonderful Life" that they keep talking about.*

*Thank you for reading this.*

*Maverick*

Sleep will not be possible anytime tonight as I just keep reading this over and over again.

# Chapter 47

# Dr. House

Do what you feel is right in your heart

For you will be criticized anyway.

Eleanor Roosevelt

**March 21st, 2010**

Sometimes your words just need to get into the right ears.

Over and over again I have been pleading with doctors that I believe that Jess can breath on her own and does not need her trach.

I believe that Jess's trach is causing a recurring infection that keeps landing her in the hospital, and each time that this happens her risk of a serious infection increases, and eventually the trach will be her demise.

I am at Stony Brook University Hospital; Jess has another infection and a 103 fever.

I have been here for four days.

A doctor that I haven't seen before walks into Jess's room and asks me: "Is there anything that you need?"

I look him right in the eye and I reply, "Yes, I need a doctor with balls."

He laughs and says: "Did you just say that you need a doctor with balls?"

"Yes I did."

I go on to explain that I believe that Jess can breath on her own without her trach, and that no doctor is willing to put his neck on the line in case something bad happens.

That my fear is that something bad is going to happen with the trach in, it is just a matter of time. That I would sign any release form or waiver taking full responsibility and exonerating all liability from the doctor who approves taking Jess's trach out.

As I am talking – the doctor puts his hand up, as if giving me a sign to stop pleading my case.

He walks out of the room.

I can see through the window of the room that he calls over two of his colleagues.

There is a heated argument that pursues.

He walks back into the room and says, "It will be out in five minutes."

I say: "Thank you Dr. House."

He laughs and walks out of the room with a fake limp.

# Chapter 48

# Lost

# Oceanic Flight 815

From the ashes a fire shall be woken,
A light from the shadows shall spring;
Renewed shall be blade that was broken,
The crownless again shall be king.


J.R.R. Tolkien

The Fellowship of the Ring

In the opening scene of the Pilot episode of "Lost", Jack Shephard opens his eyes to realize that he is injured laying flat on his back after his world has crashed.

Literally.

He survived the plane crash of Oceanic Flight 815, and now finds himself alone, with his fellow survivors on a deserted island.

As he comes too, he gets to his feet, runs though the jungle to see the beautiful ocean to his right and Armageddon from the plane crash to his left.

Instinctively, due to his training as a surgeon, he runs to the left toward Armageddon.

Understanding the magnitude of the danger that is looming he goes into his "life saving mode" and helps people avert every unforeseen possible catastrophe imaginable.

After he did as much as he could do for the day, he then retreats to a quiet area beyond the beach and tends to his own injuries.

One day after surviving the crash and becoming acquainted to his new found "home", Jack and a few other survivors head out onto the deserted island seeking help.

They find a radio transmitter.

Excitedly they turn it on and try to transmit an SOS message.

To their dismay the radio is transmitting a message in French on an endless loop that when translated says:

*"I'm alone now.*
*I'm on an island all alone.*
*Please someone come."*

One of the survivor's who has a military background and is familiar with radio transmitters determines that this message has been on an endless loop for the last 16 years.

They realize then, that no one is coming.

**April 1st, 2010**

I am lying on my back, on a mattress, which is on my living room floor.

I have taken the mattress from Jess's bed upstairs.

It is now part of my daily routine. I now use it to lie next to her hospital bed, where she sleeps, in the middle of my living room.

Jess's bed is raised off of the ground by about three feet.

I am looking up at her.

I don't sleep.

I lie wide-awake watching her.

It has been over almost three months since she has been home.

I have survived the crash of my life and I have the sudden realization that:

*I am alone now.*
*I'm on an island all alone.*

And I say to myself:

*Please someone come.*

Lying on this mattress at night, next to Jess, has become my quiet area, beyond the reach of the world, where I attend to my own injuries.

It is also the place where I realize that no one is coming to save me.

Except me.

It is a striking realization – when you realize that no one is coming to save you.

It is also the most valuable realization that you can ever have.

It is when you find your real self.

Fight or flight.

I will always choose fight.

So when the sun comes up, and the sound of cars on the road starts to trickle into my background noise every new morning, I realize that life goes on.

It is time to fight again.

And for that opportunity, I am grateful.

*"We are fighters and we know how to win."*

# Chapter 49

# Chinese Handcuffs

Nothing negative will ever come from being positive.

Nothing positive will ever come from being negative.

When your life is in Chinese handcuffs, when you feel that you are trying your hardest and your world is only getting tighter, you just need to bring yourself down to your lowest common denominator.

Just breathe.

That's it - that's all for the day.

Just breathe.

Just breathe.

Get still.

Be smarter than the trap.

Find your spot.

Everyone has his or her spot.

The place that they feel most comfortable.

The place where life is simple.

The place where you can just be.

Where the goodness of life is hiding in plain sight.

Find that spot.

My spot happens to be on an athletic field, somewhere, anywhere watching my kids train to become better athletes, which I hope and believe will translate into them becoming better people.

Those two hours of each day is the center of my cinnamon bun.

The sweet spot of life.

The piece that I savor and can eat endlessly.

So if you ever need to find me, just look in a dugout, a stinky gym or on an open field of green grass.

That is where the real me will be.

# Chapter 50

# Why Do You Wrestle?

It ain't the six minutes,
It's what happens in that six minutes.

Elmo
Vision Quest

**August 29th, 2010**

Yesterday, while I was on the side of the mat next to some wrestlers who were warming up for their next match, I found myself standing side by side next to an extraordinary wrestler.

He was warming up and he had that look of desperation on his face that wrestlers get when their match is about to start and their coach is across the gym coaching on another mat, in a match that is already in progress.

"Hey, do you have a coach?" I asked him.

"He's not here right now," he quietly answered me ready to take on the task of wrestling his opponent alone.

"Would you mind if I coached you?"

His face tilted up at me with a slight smile and said: "That would be great."

Through the sounds of whistles and yelling fans I heard him ask me "What is your name?"

"My name is John," I replied.

"Hi John, I am Nishan," he said while extending his hand for a handshake.

He paused for a second and then he said to me:
"John I am going to lose this match."

He said that as if he was preparing me so I wouldn't get hurt when my coaching skills didn't work magic on him today.

I said: "Nishan – It is not the outcome of a match that makes you a winner. You are a winner by stepping onto that mat."

With that he just smiled and slowly ran onto the mat, ready for battle, but half knowing what the probable outcome would be.

When you first see Nishan you will notice that his legs are frail - very frail. So frail that they have to be supported by custom made, form fitted braces to help support and straighten his limbs.

Braces that I recognize all to well.

Some would say Nishan has a handicap.

I say that he has a gift.

To me the word "handicap" is a word that describes what one "can't do."

That doesn't describe Nishan.

Nishan is doing.

The word "gift" is a word that describes something of value that you give to others.

And without knowing it, Nishan is giving us all a gift.

I believe Nishan's gift is inspiration.

The ability to look the odds in the eye and say: "You don't pertain to me."

The ability to keep moving forward.

Perseverance.

A "whatever it takes" attitude.

As he predicted, the outcome of his match wasn't great. That is, if the only thing you judge a wrestling match by is the final score.

Nishan tried as hard as he could, but he couldn't overcome the twenty-six pound weight difference that he was giving up to his opponent on this day in order to compete.

You see, Nishan weighs only 80 pounds and the lowest weight class in this tournament was 106.

Nishan knew he was spotting his opponent 26 pounds going into every match on this day.

He wrestled anyway.

I never did get the chance to ask him why he wrestles, but if I had to guess I would say, after watching him all day long, that Nishan wrestles for the same reasons that we all wrestle for.

We wrestle to feel alive, to push ourselves to our mental, physical and emotional limits - levels we never knew we could reach.

We wrestle to learn to use 100% of what we have today in hopes that our maximum today, will only be our minimum tomorrow.

We wrestle to measure where we started from, to know where we are now, and to plan on getting where we want to be in the future.

We wrestle to look the seemingly insurmountable opponent right in the eye and say: "Bring it on - I can take whatever you can dish out."

Sometimes life is your opponent and just showing up is a victory.

You don't need to score more points than your opponent in order to accomplish that.

No, Nishan didn't score more points than any of his opponents on this day, that would have been nice, but I don't believe that was the most important thing to Nishan. Without knowing for sure - the most important thing to him on this day was to walk with pride like a wrestler up to a thirty two foot circle, have all eyes from the crowd on him, to watch him compete one on one, not only against his opponent, but against himself and all that life has thrown at him, and in the process giving it all that he had.

That is what competition is all about.

Most of the times in wrestling you are competing against yourself.

Nishan is no different.

They say 80% of life is just showing up.

Nishan showed up today.

He showed up when most of us would have stayed in the stands.

Today all of Nishan's opponents may have scored more points than him, but he competed.

He competed against his opponents, he competed against himself and he competed against life.

And no matter what the score may have said in any one of his matches - he won in every case.

You learn later in life how important the disciplines of wrestling are to you in handling real life problems, especially when facing a seemingly insurmountable opponent in a disease or illness.

If you live long enough, life will throw you to your back.

And when it does - you are much better off if you have had wrestled.

You will know how to fight like hell to get off of your back, to get back on your feet and to come back and win.

Chances are that I probably will never see Nishan again.

That is just how life works.

"Wrestling brother" keep moving forward.

And I thank you for the gift.

You are an inspiration.

# Chapter 51

# Maybe

Not for ourselves alone are we born.

Cicero

**February 12th, 2012**

A year ago, Maverick's main competition to win a Section XI Championship came from Hauppauge's, Nick Mauriello.

The two were scheduled to wrestle a few weeks before the post season in a dual meet match between Eastport South Manor and Hauppauge High School.

It was a highly anticipated match between the two juniors; the type of match that one trains for with a little more focus, drive and determination.

The match was going be a preview of the upcoming post season.

The day arrived.

As is the case with most featured matches, it would be the last match of the day.

As each of the preceding fourteen matches came to a close, the anticipation of Mauriello vs. Passaro grew to a crescendo.

Finally it was time to wrestle.

The match never took place.

At the time we shook it off as the usual strategy that most coaches have of not wanting their wrestler to meet their main opponent so close to the Sectional Tournament.

A few days later, rumors started to leak out that Nick might be hurt. Something about Nick's knee, then his neck, circulated throughout the tight knit Long Island wrestling community.

The rumors proved to be wrong.

It was more than that.

Nick had contracted MRSA.

Methicillin-resistant Staphyloccus, or MRSA, is a bacterial infection that can be passed along through contact sports like wrestling. MRSA is a skin infection, one that if it enters your blood through an open cut, can be life threatening.

A week ago, while competing in a tournament, Nick had an open cut on his knee – it is thought that the infection entered there and then.

Whenever, and wherever he contracted it is unimportant, as the MRSA quickly and unsuspectingly circulated through Nick's bloodstream.

First it was an inflamed knee, then a stiff neck, and then within days Nick found himself at Stony Brook University Hospital on life support.

For nineteen days Nick stared death in the face.

The only good part about MRSA picking a fight with Nick was the fact that Nick was a wrestler.

*Wrestlers know how to fight.*

*Wrestlers know how to win.*

Thankfully, Nick fought and won the biggest battle of his life.

He was happy and lucky to be alive.

Four months later Nick started training again.

He started to compete again.

He started to pursue winning a Section XI Championship again.

This time, instead of being Nick's competition, Maverick became his workout partner.

A great workout partner knows when to push, and just as importantly, knows when to ease up a little so progress can be made, confidence can be built, and new levels can be achieved.

For four months Nick and Maverick trained together to prepare to win a Section XI Championship in Suffolk County, NY at 126 & 132 pounds respectively.

On February 12th, 2009 Maverick and Nick's partnership paid off as they both won a Section XI Championship; a championship which would earn each of them the right to compete for their ultimate goal, a New York State Title.

Maybe it was that in the back of their minds last year they each knew that they were going to be pushed by a great competitor, one that they both realized needed for them to be at their best to face and conquer.

Maybe that future inevitable clash drove them both to prepare to their fullest capabilities.

Maybe it was that no great competitor wants to see their elite competition ever get hurt or sick instead of being able to compete against them.

Maybe it was the chilling series of events that put Nick on life support in a medically induced coma.
Maybe it was Maverick's first hand knowledge of what someone in a medically induced coma actually is going through.

Maybe they both knew what it meant to drive down Nichols Road heading toward Stony Brook University, and to make a right hand turn into the hospital instead of a left hand turn into the Sports Complex where the Section XI Tournament is held each year.

Maybe it was realizing that when you really prioritize things in life, that wrestling is not that important.
Maybe they knew that when you *really* prioritize things during life, that wrestling is extremely important.

Maybe they knew how much stress a medical illness can have on a family.
Maybe they knew how a medical illness could bring a family closer together.

Maybe it was hearing that a strong growing young man who once weighed one hundred and forty pounds dwindled down to one hundred and twelve pounds due to his illness.
Maybe it was the first hand knowledge that Maverick had of what that weight loss looks like on someone you love.

Maybe it was the hope of the miracle recovery.

Maybe it was knowing how much focus and desire is necessary to be able to takes life's best cheap shot and keep moving forward.

Maybe it was having the opportunity of being Nick's workout partner in the off season and seeing the recovery process take shape first hand, little by little, day after day in practice.

Maybe it was a subconsciously communicated pact that allowed Maverick to be part of Nick's recovery process, in exchange for the ability to be able to believe in the "medically impossible."

Maybe it was all of this.

Maybe it was none of this.

Whatever it was - it is undeniable.

There has been a lifetime bond that has been formed between Maverick and Nick.

Need proof?

After winning the Section XI Title tonight, Maverick chose without hesitation to find Nick Mauriello, who was warming up, ready to take the mat for his own Suffolk County title, and share with him the one thing that is most sacred to a wrestler - the "First Celebration Hug."

Maybe, just maybe, without knowing it, Nick helped Maverick more than he will ever know.

# Chapter 52

# Everything Happens For A Reason

No matter how much your heart is grieving,

If you keep on believing,

The dreams that you wish

Will come true.


Walt Disney

**March 8th, 2013**

It has been 1,152 days since we brought Jess back home.

I can't tell you that it has been easy, but I can say that it has been worth it.

My original fear that my daughter was going to die before BettyJane and myself has now been replaced with the fear that she is going to outlive us.

It turned out that Jess's seizure was overridingly caused by meningitis, which we learned by reading the hospital records many months after it occurred. While being a normal teenage girl Jess had a virus that traveled to her brain which made it swell and made the electrical circuitry of her brain overheat.

Jess has made small strides forward, has had setbacks, peaks and valleys and more strides forward.

Most importantly I know that she feels our love.

During the last 1,152 days Maverick and Travis have wrestled a combined total of over 600 matches.

I used to think that wrestling was an individual sport.

It is not.

It is a true team sport.

Your team consists of your parents, your family, your coaches, your workout partners and your supporters.

Without each of them doing their part, success is not possible.

In 2012, in his senior year, Maverick finally went to the Super 32 and became an All American, was third in the nation in technical falls, and won a New York State Championship with me present and his mom watching via the Internet at home, where she was caring for Jess.

Mavericks New York State Championship was a team effort, one that I am proud to be part of and is a true testament to the power of pursuit.

One half of "I want both" complete.

In 2011 Travis also became a High School All American, by placing 4th in the NHSCA Freshmen Nationals. In 2013, Travis was first in the nation in technical falls and third in the New York State High School Tournament.

Believe it or not I am happier that Travis took third in the State Tournament rather than first. Taking 3rd is the hardest thing to do in wrestling. In order to take third, it means that you suffered a devastating loss along the way – and you had the mental toughness and the ability to handle adversity to regroup and to keep moving forward. I already knew that Travis was a champion, now I know that he is also a rebounder. And that may be more impressive.

Cassidy is my miracle little girl. She has grown up to be a caring, loving person who is always looking to help others.
Everyday she draws a picture of a happy, optimistic, radiant world.

I can't wait for Cassidy to compete in high school sports and we are in the process of coming up with a dynamic athletic goal for her, as I feel that is an important aspect of one's life.

All I can say about BettyJane is that I am the luckiest man alive. With over six billion people in the world, the right one chose me. That is the greatest asset that a man can have in his life, a great wife, mother and friend, all in one person.

I am glad that my sons are wrestlers.

Wrestling has given back to me more than I can ever imagine.
I am very thankful.

It is a great feeling knowing that you are unbreakable, and I have wrestling to thank for that.

I look forward to each day and I can't wait to find my spot where I can do something for someone who can never repay me.

I am looking across the room at Jess in her bed, in our living room.

BettyJane is beside her and our dog Bandit is cuddled next to Jess. A memory pops up into my mind of when Cassidy wanted a dog for Christmas.

Over the years I previously told Jess "no" that she couldn't get a dog.

Something inside me was telling me to change my stance this time. I asked Jess if she would be hurt if I let Cassidy get a dog after I denied her from having one.

She was just too excited about having a dog in the house to even remember me denying her one in the past.

BettyJane secretly took Jess to go pick out a dog at the kennel.

They both agreed on one, until BettyJane noticed that the dog did not have a tail.

Jessica turned to BettyJane and said: "You're telling me that If I had something wrong with me, that you wouldn't want me?"

Needless to say, that dog Bandit is now laying next to Jess on her bed, and does so everyday.

Everything in life happens for a reason. If you listen to your inner voice you will get closer to what that reason is.

It just takes time to fully develop.

I look forward to the rest of my family's lives together and I can't wait to see the full picture when it develops.

# Chapter 53

# Member of a Secret Club

The real voyage of discovery consists

Not in seeking new landscapes

But in having new eyes.


Marcel Proust

There is a club in this world that you do not join knowingly.

One day you are just a member.

It is "The Life Changing Events Club."

The fee to join the club is hurt beyond belief, payable in full, up front for a lifetime membership.

The benefit of the club is a newfound perspective on life, and a deep understanding that you may not be happy about your current situation, but you can be happy in your current situation.

The only rule to the club is that you can never let on, not even once, that your life has completely changed.

The club does not provide a directory of its members, but when you look into a member's eye, you can tell that they too are part of the club. Members are allowed to exchange that brief eye contact that says: "I didn't know."

Being a member of this club is the last thing that anyone initially wants in their life.

Being a member of this club is the best thing that ever happens to a person in their life, and there is not a person in the club that would ever give up their membership.

If you really look and know what you are looking for you can spot the clubs members; they are the ones that provide a random act of kindness and do something for someone who can never repay them for what they have done. They are the people spreading joy and optimism and lifting people's spirits even when their own heart has been broken.

I have paid my dues; my lifetime membership arrived today, not by mail, but by a deep inner feeling that I cannot describe.

It is the best club that I never wanted to be part of.

But I am for life.

# Chapter 54

# The Realization

In the midst of hate,

I found there was, within me, an invincible love.

In the midst of tears,

I found there was, within me, an invincible smile.

In the midst of chaos,

I found there was, within me, an invincible calm.

I realized, through it all,

That…

In the midst of winter,

I found there was, within me, an invincible summer.

And that makes me happy.

For it says

That no matter how hard the world pushes against me,

Within me, there's something stronger, something better,

Pushing right back.

Albert Camus

Over the last four years I have realized that I have exactly what everyone else has.

A lifetime.

And I will be damned if I lose even one day, one hour or even one second to misery.

I ask you:

If you knew that you had one last breath - what would you say?

If you had one hour to use your limbs before you would lose the use of them forever – what would you do right now?

If you knew that you wouldn't see tomorrow, whom would you make amends with today?

If you knew you had only an hour left on this earth - what would be so pressing that you just had to do it, say it, or see it?

Well there is something that I can guarantee - that one day you will have one day, one hour and one breath left, and chances are you will not know when that time will come.

Just make sure that before that day does come, that you have said, done and experienced everything that you dream of doing.

Do it now - that is what today is for.

So pick up the phone and call an old friend that you have fallen out of touch with over some silly fight that you can't remember the details of where it all went wrong.

Get out and run a mile and use your legs, make your body sweat.

Seek out someone in your life to say you are sorry to.
I'm sure someone comes to mind.

Seek out and find someone in your life that you need to thank, and let them know the impact that they have made on your life.

Seek out someone in your life that you need to express your feelings to, and express them, even if it embarrasses you.

Especially if it embarrasses you.

Then, when that day does come, you will have inner peace.

# Chapter 55

# Today Is a Great Day To Be Alive

We choose to go to the moon in this decade

And do the other things,

Not because they are easy,

But because they are hard,

Because that goal

Will serve to organize and measure the best of our energies
and skills,

Because that challenge

Is one that we are willing to accept,

One we are unwilling to postpone,

And one,

Which we intend to win.

John F. Kennedy

I have felt things that no one should ever have to feel.

I have seen things that no one should ever have to see.

I have heard things that no one should ever have to hear.

I have been beaten down so many times that it is reflexive to get back up, immediately without any hesitation, expecting another instantaneous whack to come as soon as I do.

I get up again anyway.

I have got up off the mat more times than what should be necessary.

I know I will need to continue doing so many, many more times.

I am prepared to do so, and more, without complaint or regret.

It is outright exhausting.

I keep experiencing this pain because one life is worth it.

Life is awesome and is worth fighting for.

Even one life is worth it.

For one life to experience life again is my mission.

So I will continue to feel, see and hear things that no parent should ever have too, in order for one life to be able to experience this awesome life again.

And I ask of you, please go out of your way and make someone else's life better today.

*We are all fighters and we all know how to win.*

It is a great feeling to know that you are unbreakable.

I have wrestling to thank for that.

Excuse me now as I set out to accomplish the second half of "I want both."

It is a great day to be alive.

# NEW RELEASE NOTIFICATION

To sign up for JohnA Passaro's new release notification service, send an email with your name to johnapassaro@icloud.com

In the Subject please put – NEW RELEASE NOTIFICATION

Every time JohnA Passaro has a new release, you will receive an email notification.

# Book Reviews

If you feel that this book has touched you in a small way, or has stirred emotions inside of you that have given you a different perspective or outlook on life, I invite for you to leave a book review on Amazon.com or on iTunes.com

The Book Review doesn't need to be perfect, it just needs to be something from you letting other readers know how you feel about this book.

Just type the "6 Minutes Wrestling With Life" in the url of either site and follow the link to "Leave a Book Review."

I thank you in advance, as all book reviews are greatly appreciated.

# Contact and Author Info

The greatest intangible blessings that I have received by writing this book are from the people who have reached out to me and have shared their stories with me letting me know how this book has helped them, in some small way, through their tough times.

I cherish every email that I receive.

I encourage you to contact me.

johnapassaro@icloud.com

Twitter - @johnapassaro

http://www.JohnaPassaro.com

**For Readings and Speaking Engagements email:**

johnapassaro@icloud.com

# Excerpt From

# "Again"

## The Sequel to "6 Minutes Wrestling With Life"

# Chapter 1

# Suffern

The wound is the place where the light enters you.


Rumi

Four and a half years ago, while on my way to visit with my daughter Jessica at the Helen Hayes Brain Rehabilitation Center upstate, I drove past a sign that read:

"You Are Now Entering the Town of Suffern."

The funny part is on the way back I never saw the sign that said:

"You Are Now Leaving the Town of Suffern."

That is because I never left.

I have been in suffering every day for the last 1,642 days.

There is a fight inside of me that occurs everyday between the part that just wants this ride to stop and the wrestler in me that is willing and able to take an unbelievable amount of physical and mental punishment for the ultimate reward of which the odds of achieving are so minuscule, that sanity is no longer my friend.

Luckily the wrestler in me always wins.

My friend Scott Green, the Head Wrestling Coach at Wyoming Seminary said:

*That life is 90% reason, rationality, discipline and organization.*

*You need to live your life that way.*

*That last 10% is a leap of faith, an emotional connection, an irrational belief.*

*That last 10% makes no sense at all.*

*But the truth is, nothing worth having and nothing worth accomplishing, happens without that last part.*

*You have to live in that world to do something great.*

I have been living exclusively in that world now for almost five years.

I am trying with every piece of sinew of my soul to achieve something great.

At times, it feels like I am.

At other times, it feels like I am not.

Most of the time, it just feels like Groundhogs Day, over and over again.

I keep filling my mind with success stories and I keep researching great people, trying to make sure that I have enough inspirational gas in my tank to make this whole trip.

I keep pursuing my dream and dual goal to "care for and cure" Jess and to "live and love life."

That is the reward of living in that 10%, the ability to keep plugging along as if great strides have been seen.

That is my formula, to live in that 10%, it is the only formula that I know.

So each day I win another round of my inner fight and I execute my formula of time, perseverance and an unwavering faith and belief, while taking and absorbing all punishment in the process.

As each new day starts, I feel like a Whac-A-Mole sticking my head out of the hole, time and time again, willing and able to take the shot in the head with the hopes that one day I will stick my head out of the hole, and I will no longer have to get a grief concussion.

Until then, I will leap into that 10% of life with an emotional commitment and an irrational belief, that something great is about to occur.

But first, I must shake this nagging feeling, that something is seriously wrong.

# Gift It Forward

# Campaign

If you have a few friends, a team, a classroom or an organization that you feel could benefit from "6 Minutes Wrestling With Life's" message, please consider our "Gift It Forward" campaign; where you can gift this book (at a deeply discounted price) to the people, teams, classroom or organization of your choice.

It is a great way of passing along happiness and a new perspective on life to someone close to you, no matter what they may be going through.

For more information, please email johnapassaro@icloud.com